HOW TO WORK WITH
JERKS

Getting ~~Shit~~ Stuff Done
with People You
Can't Stand

PRAISE FOR
HOW TO WORK WITH JERKS

"Jerks are everywhere! Dealing with the "work jerk" can be a taxing experience, but with this book, Eric Williamson provides readers with practical solutions for conflict management that are effective and productive. Don't let jerks mess with your mojo!"

Jeffrey Hayzlett
Primetime TV & Podcast Host; Speaker;
Author and Part-Time Cowboy

"This book is your 21st Century road map for getting things done while working with somebody you don't even want to be around at all."

Craig Valentine, MBA
World Champion of Public Speaking;
Founder, Speak and Prosper Academy

"*How to Work with Jerks* is a survival guide for the 21st century! The author not only shows us how to communicate effectively with jerks, but also what we need to do in order to not become one of the jerks! This book addresses how technology has driven communication and, at times, caused human interaction to suffer. Read this book and learn how to be a success in spite of the jerks!"

Lois Creamer
Author of *Book More Business*

"Eric provides a thoughtful and persuasive message about why managing relationships with everyone is critical to your career success."

Claudio Toyama

CEO, Toyama & Co.; Author of the #1 International Best-Seller *The Samurai Samba Vinci Way: How to Improve Your Executive Presence, Increase Trust and Lead Your Team at a World-Class Level*

"Eric's three-step process for managing conflict is essential to improving workplace relationships, productivity, and morale."

S. Andrew Musoke

Former Vice President at JPMorgan; Harvard MBA African Diaspora for Development (ADD) Representative to USA

"When I was a financial advisor, I worked for someone who was more than a jerk. If I had Eric's ideas then, the relationship would've been much different. Buy this book and save yourself the pain, frustration and aggravation of toxic business relationships. More importantly, you'll have a blueprint to create the best possible professional atmosphere with everyone around you. Well done, Eric!"

Michael Davis

Your Public Speaking MD; Author of *THE Book on Storytelling*

"From generational differences to something as simple as fostering rapport among your team, this is a great roadmap for both employees and managers. What gives this book an edge above others is Eric was able to incorporate his true, raw, real-world experience while in corporate America. The insight Eric provides will help individuals at all levels in any organization. As an HR professional, I would love to take some of these tools and implement with my own team."

Bianca Mercer
HR Director

"Being a fan and applier of non-traditional titles, I knew I would like the book as soon as I read the cover. It did not disappoint. Eric provides great insight that makes you stop, think and look for things you can change in yourself. In other words, Assess, Analyze and Act."

Aaron Beverly
1st Runner Up, 2016 World Champion of Public Speaking

"Eric provides an honest look into his journey from workplace jerk to team player and delivers a persuasive message about why managing relationships with everyone is critical to your career success."

Aisha D. DaCosta
Founder and CEO, I AM O'Kah! Inc.

"Eric does an incredible job of mixing research and personal stories to deliver a compelling message. He shows you how to increase your self-awareness in the workplace through his authenticity and vulnerability. He teaches you how to effectively handle jerks and all sorts of difficult people, and how to not become a jerk yourself. This book needs to be distributed to every company in the world."

Jeff Davis
Author of *The Power of Authentic Leadership*

"Rise above the fray with Eric's new book!"

John A. Palumbo
Author of *Highly Influential*

"Eric was studying emotional intelligence long before it was widely understood as the key factor for career performance. His three-step process to building and managing healthy relationships will help you achieve harmony and productivity in the workplace."

Randi Hogan
Fundraising Executive

"It's all about relationships and this book gives it to you straight on how to successfully manage relationships regardless of the situation. Read this book!"

Debra Cancro
Founder & CEO, VoiceVibes, Inc.

"Eric's three-step process for dealing with jerks, in the heat of the moment, will help you not to say or do something you will regret! In a verbal fight, it's the person who keeps their cool who gets what they want. This process will help you to keep your cool and not be bullied by a jerk."

Ed Tate
CSP-Certified Speaking Professional and
World Champion of Public Speaking

"Life is all about relationships! You can't do anything in this world without dealing with people, and life doesn't give us a 'how to' on relationships. This book gives you clarity on how to successfully manage relationships regardless of the situation. Read this book!"

Andy Rosas
Co-founder of How2Guys.com

HOW TO WORK WITH

JERKS

Getting ~~Shit~~ Stuff Done
with People You
Can't Stand

ERIC L. WILLIAMSON

How to Work with Jerks: Getting Stuff Done with People You Can't Stand

Published by Silver Tree Publishing, a division of Silver Tree Communications, LLC (Kenosha, WI).
www.SilverTreeCommunications.com

Editing by:
Kate Colbert, Silver Tree Publishing
JoAnn Collins, Twin Tweaks Editing

Cover design and typesetting by:
Courtney Hudson

First edition, March 2018

ISBN: 978-0-9994566-9-9

Library of Congress Control Number: 2018932242

Created in the United States of America

DEDICATION

I dedicate this book to my wife, Aleah, who always believed in me.
She is the brains behind Tailored Training Solutions. I don't make
a move without getting insight from her. I am forever grateful to her.
Aleah has supported me through all my failures and frustrations, and
is the reason for all my success. She was the first one who encouraged
me to write what I know, so that I can help others succeed. And here
we are, two years later ... I finally did it and am so proud to publish
this book.

Thank you, sweetheart ... I love you!

TABLE OF CONTENTS

FOREWORD

I would not win a contest for the title "Worked with the Most Jerks in a Lifetime." However, in a competition for most hours spent listening to people suffering the effects of workplace incivility, I would finish near the top. Having served for 15 years as an executive coach and employee assistance professional at a major university and health center that employs more than 20,000 people, I hear colleagues complain about jerks at work about four hours per day. Although I help with a range of coaching and clinical issues, I have always been a magnet for jerk fallout. I tell people constantly, **"The characters are out there."** (I was trained to avoid the word "jerk," but it's a more honest and accurate term, and Eric Williamson will tell you all about the different types.) Furthermore, the jerks exist at all levels, so climbing a career ladder won't protect you. It is only a matter of time until you work alongside, opposite, under or over a jerk at work.

When I break the news that work jerks are everywhere, some people react with shock and dismay. Being young or really lucky, they haven't yet experienced mean, disruptive or unreasonable people in professional settings, and think their current dilemma is an anomaly. The naïve expectation that workplaces are predominantly professional and reasonable is an expectation that sets them up for disillusionment. They come into their job thinking, *I am talented, hardworking and ambitious. I am*

going to pour my heart into this job, make significant contribu-
tions and improve some existing systems. When people see my
accomplishments, they will like me, respect me, and eventually
cry at my promotion or retirement party.

That was my mindset when I started my career as a clinical
social worker. I thought my supervisors and administrators,
being in the business of helping people suffering poverty and
mental illness, must be pretty cool. As it turned out, those
social workers were sadistic and incompetent. This book
disrupts the fantasy that any profession or work environment
may be immune from jerks, and confronts the faulty assump-
tion that talent and work ethic can create long-term career
success without attention to managing conflict and nurturing
workplace relationships.

Once people accept that work jerks abound, they can start
re-writing the narratives that take them off course — the first
being that they can quit and find a new, jerk-free position.
I have lost count of clients who tired of their tormentors, left
their department, then called me a year later with a new workplace relationship problem. Unfortunately, running away from
jerks usually leads to what Michael Douglas's character in *Wall
Street* called "a dog with different fleas."

People also erroneously believe they can overpower jerks with
righteousness, thinking, *They're wrong, I'm right, and I'm going
to get management and HR to see it my way and make them
stop being jerks.* Unfortunately, their adversaries are thinking
the same thing! Then, everyone digs in, factions form and the
aggrieved often make *themselves* jerks in the process. People
who are self-reflective or open to feedback often recognize

their own evolution to work jerk, including this book's author! Ultimately, the notion of being "right" is not relevant to career success, creates no resolution, can turn good people into momentary characters, and creates a hot mess of drama, conflict, distraction and expense.

Discarding the erroneous assumptions that you can avoid or defeat jerks at work leads to a truer, more empowering belief: **you must be prepared to coexist with jerks and manage workplace relationships at all times throughout your career, no matter your rank.** If you are in leadership, you have a critical decision to make: try to control or get rid of the jerks (which I've argued won't work); do nothing and resign your organization to the scourge of conflict, turnover, and low morale; or use the author's AAA/ 5-Star methods to weave rationality, effective communication and civility into work-place culture.

Even if you have found your dream job with the ideal boss or partner, that person could move, retire, get fired or tragically die tomorrow, and his or her replacement could turn your world upside down, overnight. I have seen it happen many times. It has happened to me. No worries — Eric Williamson has a book for that.

Jason Sackett, PCC, LCSW, CEAP
Executive Coach
Coach Supervisor
Training facilitator of *Managing Upset*
Author of *Compassion@Work:*
Creating Workplaces that Engage the Human Spirit

PROLOGUE

HOW THIS BOOK BENEFITS YOU

Congratulations! You have made a wise and important invest-ment by purchasing this book. *How to Work with Jerks* will serve as your training guide for dealing with jerks so that you can succeed in the workplace. This book was written to inform its readers — employees, business leaders and people of all generations interested in career success — how to work with jerks so that you can survive and *thrive* in today's ever-changing work environment. This book is also for employers, business leaders, and entrepreneurs who are seeking solutions to retain and leverage their top talent and connect with their staff. This book is for Millennials, Baby boomers, Generation Xers, and iGen'ers (also known as Gen Z) in the workforce, or poised to enter the workforce, who need to work together to solve prob-lems and get work done.

This book provides solutions sought by professionals and leaders about how to motivate and retain their staff and continue getting the maximum productivity out of them. This book also answers the questions asked by all employees about how to stay motivated in a job they can't stand while learning the necessary skills to make them marketable in today's uncertain job market. Regardless of the generation to which you belong, you will gain skills that will help you earn promotions, work well with others and become more marketable. You will gain the confidence and skill sets to pursue and achieve your dreams while managing stress along the way.

WHAT YOU WILL LEARN AND APPLY

You will learn something unique and special that will immediately improve your relationships with the people you can't stand ... or who can't stand you. Specifically, after reading this book and putting its insights into practice, you will have:

- Improved performance, communication and job opportunities
- Improved relationships with your colleagues, friends and family and
- Reduced stress.

In this book, I share details about the various leadership characteristics I learned first-hand from my experiences. You'll learn to apply that understanding to help you in your own career, and you will also learn about solutions to common problems we experience in the workplace. I will share training techniques, and stories of effective and ineffective leadership using examples from both the public and private sectors. This book contains activities in each chapter to help you immediately apply what you have learned. You will understand why it matters to change your leadership style when dealing with conflict and exactly how to do it. You will learn about what it takes to step outside your comfort zone to achieve success and tap into your full potential.

I was born in 1980, which makes me a Millennial. Having worked and managed Millennials and other generations for more than 15 years, I understand what motivates us and makes us unique, but more importantly, I also understand what all generations in the workforce truly need in order to thrive in today's work environment. My leadership experience and tools shared throughout the book will not only help Millennials, but are intended to help all generations overcome the relationship challenges that make it difficult and sometimes impossible to work with jerks. Learning how to more effectively deal with difficult people and situations can help advance your career and reduce your stress.

SECTION ONE

UNDERSTANDING JERKS IN THE WORKPLACE – THE BASICS

HOW I BECAME A WORK JERK

Like you, I have seen the word "success" defined in many ways. Does it take good grades and education, high IQ scores and standardized tests, climbing up the corporate ladder, and playing politics? Is it about good timing and good luck? Is it only meant for a select few? Or is there a different story?

Through my travels around the world, along with almost two decades of leadership experience, and working in various types of work environments, my belief is that success is about stepping outside your comfort zone — that it's not about privilege, circumstance or upbringing.

> Success is deliberate, does not discriminate, is not accidental and cannot be measured relative to someone else. More importantly, success in the work environment is about how well you interact and build relationships with others.

But when I began working at my first job, success was hard to come by. My success in school did not immediately translate to success at work because I was unprepared. I lacked the professional maturity and the appropriate social skills to interact with others, particularly the more seasoned employees (mostly Baby Boomers) in the workforce.

I went to college in the same decade that introduced the Internet, instant messenger and other social media technology. By the time I graduated from Connecticut College in 2002, I had a GPA north of 3.0 and I received an offer letter from the very first full-time job to which I had applied. To my chagrin, little did I know I couldn't rely on good grades to be successful when I got a full-time job. My school success did not prepare me for a professional job. It comes as no surprise that my first year on the job was somewhat rocky, at best. I learned that it would take much more than good grades to succeed at work ... and I would experience the same frustrations many of you have when dealing with jerks. But I soon realized that the people I worked with thought *I* was a jerk.

TROUBLE AT WORK

"The environment I had unknowingly created was so toxic. One of two things could have and should have happened during that first year: I could've quit or I should've gotten fired."

I had trouble fitting in and getting along with my coworkers at that first job. I was the youngest person working in the office. My coworkers referred to me as "the kid." I could not relate to any of them. For example, when it was pay day, my only concern was figuring out where I was going to party during the weekend. On the other hand, my older coworkers had different priorities. They were more concerned with paying their bills on time and prioritizing family commitments, like taking their kids to soccer practice, birthday parties or dentist appointments. Among all the people in the office, I especially had difficulty getting along with my mentor. Because I was new to the job, my boss assigned me a mentor to help show me the ropes.

I initially thought my mentor was a real jerk. I thought she was rude, sarcastic and impatient. To her, I never did anything right. She used to boss me around and tell me how I should do my job. She used to say things like, "Don't do it that way, do it my way!" Our personalities clashed and I did not know how to handle it. I would lash out some- times and argue when I disagreed with her. There were times when I felt so stressed by my relationship with my mentor that I simply didn't want to work with her anymore, let alone show up to work at all. Sometimes I felt like ignoring all professional decorum, being very candid and letting her know exactly how I felt about her!

As I look back at that time in my life, I realize I lacked a certain level of maturity needed to handle these kinds of situations that occur at work. Because of all the success I had while in college — admittedly a different world from the "real world" of work — I had developed an ego, and it became my amigo. Because I did well in school, I felt like I would do well at work. In addition to my lack of maturity, I took things personally at work. When my coworkers asked me questions about an assignment, I would get defensive, thinking they doubted my abilities. I argued with them often and did not get along with most of them.

Even worse, I had trouble getting along with the people I served — the people in need of help! You see, I was working for a federal agency that administers support services like disability benefits. I considered the job truly rewarding, but there was a degree to which I also considered it a thankless job. Sure, I was in the business of helping people in need; however, it felt like it was never enough. Some people needed help because they could not work due to being disabled. As a result, they sought disability benefits to supplement their lost income. I could not help some of them receive these benefits because they did not meet the federal disability requirements to be considered disabled. No matter how hard I tried to explain why they were ineligible, some clients were frustrated and upset and they took it out on me. And how did I respond? Once again, I took it personally, got defensive and argued with them. They eventually complained to my manager about my behavior, saying I was rude and abrasive toward them.

The environment I had unknowingly created for all who had to work with me was so toxic. One of two things could have and *should have* happened during that first year: I could've quit or I should've gotten fired.

HELP FROM WHERE YOU LEAST EXPECT IT

I thought the latter scenario — me getting fired — was destined to happen when my boss summoned me to his office one winter morning with the ominous phrase, "Eric, I need to talk to you." I braced for the worst. As I made my way to his office, all I could think about were all the times I screwed up on the job and the number of times I argued with my coworkers and clients. I had a feeling in my gut that this discussion was not going to end well.

To my surprise, my boss did not immediately scold me for my poor behavior. He did not tell me to clean out my desk. Instead, he handed me a birthday card to sign for one of my coworkers. I was so relieved he was not going to fire me! However, when I signed the card and handed it back to him, he took a deep breath and said, "I realize you have had difficulty during your first year and it's affecting your performance. If you would like to continue working here, you're going to have to turn things around quickly, and here is what I am going to do to help you." I was shocked that he was offering to help me. *He was not going to fire me!* Instead, he registered me for an upcoming emotional intelligence (EQ) workshop. I had no idea what emotional intelligence was at the time; I'd never even heard the term. The only thing I knew about it was based on what my boss said in those next few minutes. He said that it would help me improve my relationships with others in the workplace. He said that by understanding my emotions, I would be able to better manage my behavior in the workplace, and that that improved EQ would help me work better with my coworkers, serve my clients more effectively, and overall, improve my performance.

My first reaction was defensive. On the surface, I did not think I was to blame for my performance issues. My ego convinced me that it was everyone else who had a problem, not me. However, I quickly realized that my boss was not giving me an option, no matter how concerned he was about my performance. My job was on the line. He basically "volun-told" me to attend this course in an effort to improve my performance. I felt compelled to attend the course out of fear of losing my job.

Ah Hah!

To my surprise, attending that emotional intelligence course opened my eyes about many things *I* was doing wrong at work. That course helped me become aware about how I respond to stressful situations in the workplace. It also helped me become aware about how poorly I treated my coworkers when they were only trying to help me. For example:

- I lashed out at my coworkers when I disagreed with them.

- I argued with my mentor when she tried to give me feedback to improve my performance.

- I got defensive toward my coworkers when they questioned my decisions.

- I got frustrated with some of my clients when they needed me for help, even though they were ineligible for disability benefits.

I continually demonstrated poor interpersonal skills toward my colleagues and clients. I lacked confidence when interacting with my coworkers, I was combative, and was often abrasive, partly because I was always feeling defensive about my work.

I realized that **I was a jerk!** I would think back to how upset and petty I acted when I was at odds with another coworker. When I realized how I was acting, I was not proud of my behavior. I had to turn things around fast, not just to save my job, but because I owed it to my coworkers, to the people I served, and to myself.

This was a pivotal moment in my life and my career.

Thanks to that EQ workshop and to a boss who believed in second chances, I got on the road to change. I learned the importance of building strong relationships with my coworkers, especially those who I did not get along with, such as my mentor and other colleagues. I realized that I can't always get work done all by myself; I have to rely on others to be successful.

I went through some workplace challenges where I dealt with people I simply could not stand. And if you're like most people, you can relate. Luckily for me, I had a boss who invested in me to take the necessary training to improve my workplace relationships and my productivity. Without him, my career at that job may not have lasted that long. Not everyone is fortunate enough to have a boss who can provide the support and resources necessary for you to do your job effectively. Some people may have to rely on the alternative option — learning on the fly. Learning on the fly is considered an important and sometimes necessary on-the-job-training method and is a great tool to learn from mistakes — about what to do and what NOT to do. But the downside to learning on the fly is that, just like it's impossible to unscramble eggs after you have already scrambled them, it's impossible to take words and actions back after you've already made a kneejerk reaction to a stressful situation. This type of training is not enough. You need an additional tool to help you with these challenges, that that's precisely why I think this book will benefit you. After reading this book and completing in the activities, you will be armed with the tools you need to work with jerks and successfully navigate through the challenges in today's ever-changing work environment.

2

WHO ARE WORK JERKS?

Like you, I have always felt grateful to have a job. But despite being grateful, have you ever had difficulty getting along with some people you have worked with? Whether they were rude, bossy, or sarcastic, these people can be jerks!

> *A work jerk is someone who does not use social skills as a necessary job skill.*

Whether they simply don't realize the importance of social skills, or whether they deny that they lack social skills, jerks make it extremely difficult for you to excel in the workplace. Additionally, they fail to manage their emotions in the workplace according to the situation, and may end up acting like a jerk toward their colleagues or making impulsive decisions without taking the time to think before acting. These people also fail to leverage workplace relationships to improve productivity, performance or morale. In addition to being rude, bossy, or sarcastic, some characteristics of work jerks include but are not limited to:

- The micromanager
- The bully
- The complainer
- The dictator

- The narcissist
- The poor communicator and listener
- The person who takes credit for your work, throws you under the bus or undermines your authority
- The person who is inflexible
- The person who creates a toxic environment of fear and distrust, and
- The person who lacks integrity or honesty.

I bet you may know some of these people, huh? You may recognize these characteristics from people you have worked with and can't stand. You may also recognize these characteristics within yourself at times, which — similar to my own situation — could be a reason why some people have trouble getting along with you. If you have other work jerk characteristics to include, feel free to add to this list by identifying other characteristics of work jerks.

WORK JERK CHARACTERISTICS

① The "Joan of Arc" (hero complex), the person who overdoes everything and feels the need to almost "invent" conflict or unfair work conditions and then begins to recruit followers for their cause in an attempt to speak for (and represent) everyone.

② "The Kiss-up" - doesn't need defining?

HOW ARE WORK JERKS PROBLEMATIC?

Whether you are a Millennial who is having difficulty getting along with a jerk who is a Baby Boomer or vice versa, the struggle is real.

When members of any team are constantly dealing with jerks who aren't willing to embrace the positive nature of generational-based differences in the workplace, it can have a real impact on the company and its people. Not only can it affect the company's bottom line, it can affect your health and well-being. Among many unfortunate outcomes, the cost of working with jerks can lead to decreased productivity, work absence and poor relationships.

Dealing with jerks makes us less productive. According to a study published by CPP, an industry leader in research, training and organizational development tools, such as the Myers-Briggs assessments, U. S employees spend up to 2.1 hours a week in conflict. Based on my experience working in both the public and private sectors, we can spend more time than that dealing with conflict just from the jerks. We may spend time figuring out how to respond to a jerk or deal with the situation at hand, complaining to others about jerks, or engaged in back and forth discussions, or tit-for-tat debates with jerks. This negative activity comes at the expense of focusing on getting our own work done. This can be taxing on your mind, as well as your body. And because it's taxing on your mind and body, some people would rather not show up to work at all. In fact, one in four people who don't show up to work are absent because of being too stressed or too sick to deal with the jerks. I'm convinced that a major component of workplace absenteeism is related to unresolved dynamics between jerks and the well-intentioned coworkers who just want to get along.

Those who don't show up to work are choosing to avoid the jerks because they don't know what else to do. Others get so fed up with dealing with jerks that they leave the company — voluntarily or involuntarily. And for employers, it can cost nearly 200% more than that employee's salary to find a replacement. Dealing with jerks also leads to poor relationships. We may not want to admit it, but we rely on others (especially jerks) to get our work done. These poor relationships cause resentment, hostility and, sadly, workplace violence. In 2017, workplace violence accounted for nearly 13% of aggravated assaults and nearly 18 % of simple assaults.

To get an idea of how you may respond to jerks or stressful situations either in the work environment or outside of work, visit my website at www.TailoredTrainingSolutions.com to complete a free self-assessment.

HOW DO WE BECOME WORK JERKS?

Let's face it ... nobody really wants to be a jerk. You may be thinking that, with all the training and resources available today, people who work together should be getting along and working cohesively. So why are there still jerks at work? Why do we have difficulty getting along with certain people? I certainly did not intend to be a jerk. So while I am convinced that nobody else intends to become a jerk, I believe there are four circumstances that play a critical role in creating an environment that inevitably becomes a haven for jerks. They are:

Circumstance #1

CONSTANT FRUSTRATION CAUSED BY SOCIAL MEDIA AND TECHNOLOGY

Social media and technology have drastically altered human interaction in the work environment, removing us from the face-to-face connection we were once used to. No matter where you work, the workplace requires you to communicate with others to get work done. You cannot do it alone. Before Millennials entered the workforce, employees had to meet face-to-face to get work done or relied heavily on the telephone. However, nowadays, thanks to improved technology, there are new, more efficient ways of doing business that don't require face-to-face meetings. In many situations, people are allowed to work in the comfort of their own homes, also known as telework or telecommuting. This minimizes the face-to-face interaction with other coworkers. What used to be accomplished in a cubicle or in a meeting room with a group of people in business attire can now be accomplished in your jeans and tees (or even pajamas!) in the comfort of your own home. Although this can make us more efficient in terms of getting work done, and also helps us achieve better work/life-balance, this change in human interaction has a real impact on how we deal with conflict while working with others. It can make us less prepared to handle conflict or participate in crucial conversations with our coworkers.

Additionally, we now rely heavily on technology, such as email, social media, and automation to get work done faster and more efficiently. This lack of human interaction stunts our interpersonal development, affecting the way we respond to situations and current events. Instead of conversing face-to-face with a coworker, we oftentimes do it electronically via email or instant messenger. There are people who literally sit next to someone at work and communicate via email instead of speaking aloud, face to face. We miss out on observing the tone, the context and the body language during face-to-face meetings — all of which can be vital to comprehension and the health of a relationship. When we rely mainly on email and other forms of technology to communicate in the workplace instead of face-to-face meetings, it creates distance among coworkers. Things can get lost in translation by relying only on email and text messages.

Can you recall a time when you sent or received an email that came off differently than intended? Instead of meeting to discuss an issue affecting a project or colleague, people would rather use email as a means to address the issue more efficiently.

This lack of human interaction affects our behavior and the way we respond to others. Managers or supervisors may find it challenging when having face-to-face conversations with their employees to address poor behavior or performance issues. Likewise, employees may find it challenging to control their emotions when having these discussions with their managers or supervisors. Additionally, they may have difficulty controlling poor behavior because they may not even realize it is a problem; if a supervisor has never addressed a behavior issue face-to-face, an employee can be left in the dark about the impact of their workplace behaviors. Although technology in the workplace helps us become more efficient and thorough, it can also be counterproductive if we don't find the right balance between leveraging technology and face-to-face interaction.

Social media has also changed how we handle conflict and face-to-face interactions. Some of us sound off on social media platforms, such as Twitter, Instagram and Facebook, expressing ourselves in front of random and anonymous people online. We may quickly react to things going on in the world or encounters we've had, and we're apt to express how we may be feeling at that moment and share it with the social media public without considering the outcome of our actions. We spend little time, if any at all, to assess the consequences of these actions — and when we do, attempting to delete a comment before anyone else can react, it is too late ... it's been seen, responded to or even shared. After we post comments to social media, it's for everyone to see. Some people have paid a terrible price with social media by losing job opportunities, getting fired or losing a promotion because of their unbecoming behavior on social media. Be sure to think before you tweet because employers take these actions seriously; whether it's true for you or not, prospective employers are likely to view your online behaviors and persona as a reflection of how you conduct yourself at work.

Circumstance #2
ONGOING ANXIETY CREATED BY LACK OF TRAINING AND PREPARATION

Unfortunately, there are many people hired into the workforce who are unprepared for their new positions. Students who graduate from college or people who have acquired their first full time job have no clue about how to adopt the necessary socials skills needed to manage workplace relationships or how to navigate through the political atmosphere embedded in the work environment. Some are unequipped to deal with the workplace challenges associated with the job and may lack the professional maturity to adjust their social skills to fit the professional mold that sometimes takes years to develop. In addition to the challenges of learning the actual job, new employees without experience and social savvy are at an immediate disadvantage and risk of not fitting in or getting along.

The same holds true for seasoned employees who transition into leadership positions. Some of these people are simply not equipped to take on these roles. Why is this? This can happen because some leaders who were hired to a leadership position were great at their former technical position, which does not always translate into solid leadership skills. Before they were promoted, they were responsible for doing the work and producing the results. They hardly had experience with leading others to produce the same results. Because of this, they may have not been able to adequately develop these skills or been able to put them into practice in their prior technical positions.

A person who is promoted because of expertise ("He's great with numbers") finds himself at a new level, where many or most duties revolve around managing people — not technical skills.

> **The working world is peppered with bad or inexperienced bosses, which explains why people are abrasive, thoughtless, and otherwise interpersonally inept in so many positions of power in organizations everywhere.**

To further illustrate this point, I am reminded of a former client in the public sector who needed my help in improving the performance of his management staff so that they could be more effective in leading and supervising their own staff. The group of managers I worked with were newly hired supervisors. They were recently promoted into their positions and had difficulty getting along with their staff and could not get them to do their work. Their staff did not respect their new management. Their staff thought they were *jerks*!

I delivered a three-day workshop that focused on three things: improving their relationship with their staff, managing conflict, and addressing performance and conduct issues that hindered office production. I also spent some time working with the management staff individually to get to know them and focus on specific areas to help them improve their management skills. One of the things that stood out the most while working with them is that, like others, they were promoted into management because they were superstars at their former positions. They had little, if any, experience in leading and motivating others to get work done. They lacked the people skills

— the interpersonal skills required to get work done through other people. In management, you have to lead others to produce results rather than doing the work yourself. This was something they were not used to.

What got you here won't get you there ...

It's true (and it's also the title of a fantastic book by executive coach Marshall Goldsmith). With luck, most people promoted from technical, tactical roles into management will quickly realize that the skills that got them into management are not the same skills that will help them excel at their new position. When it came to the group of new managers at my three-day workshop, they each needed to develop a different skillset for their position. During the time I spent with the management staff, they learned to apply some of the tools needed to connect with their staff so that they could get the maximum productivity out of them. They also learned how to deal with stressful situations, such as managing conflict and getting their staff to prioritize and meet deliverables with aggressive timelines. When I followed up with the management staff to see how they were handling their new supervisory positions, I was pleased to learn that not only had they improved their relationships with their staff, they were also able to form a relationship that directly led to improved employee performance and office production.

A few months later, I was invited to return to deliver a keynote address to the entire company on how to work with jerks. More specifically, how to get work done with the people you can't stand ... or who can't stand you. This experience helped convince the business leaders at this company that not only did their entire management team need specific training that focuses on building relationships and managing conflict in order to manage their staff effectively; but their staff also needed training to help them manage conflict and communicate more effectively with their peers and their management.

Circumstance #3
INSECURITY CAUSED BY FINANCIAL UNCERTAINTY

When companies and communities face financial hardships, jerks appear out of nowhere. Financial uncertainty creates a level of anxiety and desperation. Some people get stressed out when their company has layoffs because they are uncertain whether they will be next to lose their job. In harsh economic times, when people lose their jobs and have economic setbacks, they get frustrated with the thought of having to start all over again. The life they were once used to is gone, and during these uncertain times, the only jobs available are sometimes the ones in which they may be underpaid and/ or overworked. People become upset and bitter with the thought of working somewhere they hate, but must out of survival. These feelings can create a toxic environment of disgruntled employees in the workplace, straining the relationships needed to foster a healthy environment to get work done.

A classic example of this situation affected people on a much larger scale — the 2008 financial crisis. It was one of the biggest catastrophes that has affected all generations in today's workplace. Not only did it affect the ability of many of us to find a job or advance in our careers, it also caused major challenges in our ability to maintain healthy relationships personally and professionally. According to David Goldman's article, "Worst Year for Jobs since '45," the 2008 financial crisis resulted in more than 2.5 million job losses nationwide. It was arguably the worst recession in American history. It affected people of all generations who were entering the workforce, in the workforce or leaving the workforce. Students who graduated from college struggled to find jobs. Many employees were laid off when their companies shut down. Additionally, older employees who were poised to retire could not afford to do so and this situation forced them to stay at jobs they were otherwise ready to leave. People entering the workforce were desperate and anxious to land a job. They were willing to accept anything and everything offered to them — even if that job offered low pay, poor benefits and was far away. This led to depression, anger, frustration and resentment in systemic ways.

The 2008 financial crisis jeopardized the future for Millennials who were just entering the workforce, as well as for other generations who were already working. In 2008, Millennials like myself were up-and-coming in the workforce. At that time, we were building momentum in our careers, beginning to establish financial stability and building confidence, poised to achieve anything. Like many professionals in their prime, regardless of age or generation, it was our time to shine. However, the economic downturn affected our wellbeing and set us back to the point some doubted we would ever recover.

The 2008 financial crisis also affected older generations such as the Baby Boomers. Many of them had plans to retire after working 30 or more years. While some had plans after retirement to travel, take on a hobby or invest in their own small business, the economic uncertainty disrupted those plans. Retirement pensions were not enough. Some had to continue working to ensure they could pay their mortgage and keep up with their bills. Others were forced to continue working to support their children or even grandchildren who are unemployed.

Economic uncertainty can create feelings of frustration and anxiety, and can contribute to toxic work environments. Whether it's a major crisis like 2008 or just a period where job availability is limited, difficult financial times can stress people out, making it nearly impossible to build healthy, lasting work relationships.

> In the aftermath of financial havoc, work environments are inevitably over-run with jerks.

Circumstance #4
CONTINUOUS STRESS DUE TO A LACK OF GENERATIONAL AWARENESS

Today's work environment consists of multiple generations. While this should help contribute to a healthy and diverse work environment, it can also contribute to toxic work environments, misunderstandings and jerks at work. This is because we may fail to acknowledge the types of people we work with, or fail to adjust our working style to suit the types of people above, below or alongside us at work.

If you are currently employed or expect to be in the near future, there is a strong chance that you will work in a multi-generational environment consisting of Millennials, Generation Xers, Baby Boomers, and eventually iGen'ers. These generations represent today's workforce.

People in the workforce need to gain a deeper understanding of each other's challenges and goals, in order to work productively together. Together, these generations can thrive in a professional environment, but it requires more than just education and technical experience to succeed. We all must learn how to manage and maneuver around toxic work environments and deal with people from different generations who have different personalities, behaviors and experience. Not dealing with these situations the right way can cause stress, unhappiness and employee turnover. Knowing that, let's jump right into Chapter 5 to review these generations to get a better understanding of what we all bring to the table in the work environment and how different perspectives can lead us to butt heads.

GENERATIONS IN THE WORKFORCE

BABY BOOMERS

Baby Boomers are people born between the years 1946 and 1964.
According to the U.S. Census Bureau, they are labeled as "Baby
Boomers" because during this period, there was a significant increase
in the number of births that occurred. According to author Gary
Gilles, who completed a study titled "What are Baby Boomers?,"
1946 was the beginning of the "boom." In that one-year period alone,
3.4 million babies were born in the U.S., which was, at the time, the
most births ever in a one-year period in the United States. Each year
from 1953 to1964, that annual number of 3.4 million increased to
approximately 4 million babies born each year. By the end of 1964,
76.4 million people had born. In a 22-year period, one-quarter of
the U.S. population had been born. The world and the economy had
been changed forever.

Assigning common characteristics to entire generations is fraught
with risk, but few people would argue Baby Boomers have earned
a reputation for having a strong work ethic. And there is something
about having a hard day's work that makes their day complete.
Typically, Boomers can work independently and don't need a "pat on
the back" for doing their job. Their strong appreciation for working

hard and paying their dues before climbing up the corporate ladder can make them act like jerks when dealing with other generations who view work differently. For example, other generations who value more workplace flexibility and work/life-balance may work hard but seek instant gratification from their employer or expect a promotion after working only a short period of time. Boomers simply can't relate.

GENERATION X

People who represent Generation X were born roughly between 1965 and 1980. This generation is in between the Baby Boomer and Millennial generations. This generation is also known as the "latchkey generation" because their parents often left them alone while they worked, and they were the first generation to carry house keys around their necks or in their book bags. Members of this generation are known to be productive workers, respecting authority (although not impressed with titles), and enjoy work life-balance and flexible hours. Some people in this generation may be perceived as jerks because of their emphasis toward achieving work-life balance, sometimes in tradeoff to focusing on climbing the corporate ladder.

MILLENNIALS

Millennials, also known as Generation Y, represent children born roughly between 1980 and 2002. They make up the largest generation in the U.S., representing approximately 80 million children. This generation will replace the Baby Boomer generation when Boomers finish retiring. Millennials are the most educated generation to date, holding the largest number of bachelor's degrees, master's degrees, doctoral degrees and other professional degrees. They are known for being extremely technology savvy. For those of you who are not Millennials, I want to provide a bit more details about this generation and our impact on today's work environment.

Millennials like myself have been taught to follow their dreams and possess a heightened level of confidence that they can follow their dreams. This sense of confidence keeps us from becoming complacent too quickly. We want to be challenged and want our ideas to be taken seriously. We seek feedback early and often. While other generations, such as the Baby Boomers are willing to pay their dues and work several years at a position before climbing up the corporate ladder, or do something they love, Millennials see instant success as something very attainable. This way of thinking can make us be perceived as jerks because it may differ with how most work environments are managed. Due to the ever-changing business environment, some employers, who may be older, believe that we need to better prepare Millennials and younger generations entering the workforce if organizations are going to be optimally successful. Because Millennials represent the largest generation in the workforce today, let's spend some time to closely examine this generation so we can have a better understanding of their impact.

MILLENNIALS IN THE WORKFORCE

The US Bureau of Labor Statistics predicts that Millennials will make up approximately 75% of the workforce by 2030. Employers will need to gain a better understanding of them in order to leverage their talents in the workplace, contribute to a healthy working relationship, and position their companies for present and future success.

Millennials are eager to succeed, hungry to make a difference and confident in their abilities to make an impact. This generation is unlike any other that has hit the employment market and is the largest generation to hit the job market since the Baby Boomers. The sheer volume of Millennials, combined with the relative lack of Gen Xers and the increasing retirement of Baby Boomers, means that employers will be facing leadership gaps. Moreover, they will be looking to Millennials to fill those gaps, which is why — according to business consultants Jessica Brack and Kelly Kip — employers will need to learn to manage this generation, and this generation will need to learn how to thrive in the work environment.

> *"... they might be less experienced and more frustrated than previous generations."*

Dan Schawbel, founder of Millennial Branding and author of *Promote Yourself,* finds that Millennials are more likely to be living with their parents, unable to achieve financial independence, and even those who have higher degrees are often underemployed. He adds that companies need to understand these issues because when Millennials are hired, they might be less experienced and more frustrated than previous generations. The source of their frustration is that Millennials, like myself, have high expectations that may not be realistic for most employers. This means that right from the beginning, there is a difference in expectations between Millennials and their employers, which must be addressed. And what complicates matters for Millennials in the workforce is that most of us **don't believe we should be expected to stay with any employer more than a year.** This goes against what many, if not all, employers believe and expect from their staff. For most employers, hiring an employee is considered a long-term investment. For Millennials, the career path can be winding and is about seeking new challenges and opportunities, even if that means changing employers again and again. As you can see, this situation can present a conflict where both sides may consider each other jerks.

SECTION TWO

LEARNING HOW TO WORK WITH JERKS (AND AVOID BECOMING ONE YOURSELF)

THE SOLUTION TO DEALING WITH WORK JERKS

So how can we prevent fallout from jerk behavior in the workplace if we can't simply get rid of all the jerks? How can we work better with jerks, become happier, less stressed and more productive? Despite common practice, or what you may have experienced yourself, the answer is NOT:

- Avoiding them
- Telling a jerk exactly how you feel about them, and/or
- Violent behavior: lashing out and causing some physical harm to someone.

These options only help you become a jerk yourself! This only makes matters worse. Avoiding situations where jerks are present inadvertently sends a message that jerk behavior is acceptable and does not bother you. And it is only a matter of time before you blow up at that person. Trust me, you do not want that to happen because that's how I became a jerk when I got my first job. Instead, use my **AAA Method and the 5 Star Traits** when working with jerks and handling stressful situations in the workplace.

A THREE-STEP PROCESS TO DEALING WITH JERKS: AAA METHOD – ASSESS, ANALYZE, ACT

I will be the first to admit that I had more than my fair share of allowing my emotions to get the best of me, causing me to make rash decisions. While these experiences caused me to act like a jerk, it also cost me job opportunities, soured relationships and made some bad situations worse. I made it my purpose to help others from going through the same mistakes.

When dealing with conflict from jerks, we often have the tendency to let our emotions get the best of us and we can react without considering the consequences of our actions. This not only makes a bad situation worse; it causes us to behave like a jerk too! Instead of making an impulsive decision when engaged in a heated discussion, we need to take a more measured approach, demonstrate poise and respond thoughtfully and professionally. This may sound easier said than done; however, this is possible. In fact, I have created a three-step process that not only helps you manage tough situations, it also improves relationships with others and, more importantly, helps you work better with the people you can't stand, especially jerks. I call it the **AAA Method: Assess, Analyze, Act**.

Participants in my training workshops have found tremendous value when using the AAA Method to deal with conflict in the workplace.

But the only way it works is through practice. It requires a conscious effort to employ these steps while in conflict.

Step 1: Assess the situation. When dealing with conflict at work or in your personal life, it is important to assess the situation. This involves not only being aware of your emotions and how you are feeling, but how the other person is feeling.

Reflect on a specific situation you have experienced to identify these emotions. What does your behavior or body language signal to the other person? What behavior or body language does that person signal to you? Sometimes when we are stressed or dealing with a difficult situation, we can exhibit at least one or more of the following reactions. Our heart may beat fast, we can get shortness of breath, we may clinch up or our palms may become sweaty. How do *you* respond?

Not only should you be aware of your body gestures and other's body gestures, you should also be aware of the current situation or the circumstance. For example:

- Are you stressed because you have an immediate deadline you are struggling to meet?
- Are there multiple things going on at the same time that may be overwhelming and you may be unsure which priority to tackle first?

Step 2: Analyze the situation. Once you have assessed the situation and are aware of what your emotions and behaviors are signaling to others, the next step is to analyze your emotions and behaviors. Determine why you are feeling stressed. What situation has occurred that has caused you to feel stressed? Additionally, seek to understand

and reflect on the thoughts and feelings of the other person involved. For example:

- Why is the other person acting rude or abrasive toward you?
- What situation(s) has occurred that has caused you both to be stressed?

Step 3: Act. Once you have a full understanding of the situation (meaning you are aware of what has caused you or the other person to be stressed and you understand what may be contributing to these feelings), you can respond and act most appropriately. This is one of the most important steps because it prevents you from allowing your emotions to get the best of you and keeps you from making an impulsive decision you will most likely regret.

Remember, in conflict, we cannot always be right. When you take the time to assess and analyze the situation, you may determine you are in the wrong, which may require you to apologize or adjust your response.

The AAA Method must be practiced repeatedly for you to become a master at working better with jerks. Many times, when we are caught up in the heat of the moment, we skip directly to Step 3 and act based on how we are feeling at that moment. This causes more problems, including jeopardizing your career and worsening the relationship with the other person. Following this process and tackling the steps *in order* will help you communicate more effectively with all generations in the workforce, mitigate conflict before it comes to a head and prevent you from making a rash decision that you may regret.

PREVENT MAKING KNEEJERK REACTIONS

Practice the Assess-Analyze-Act Method

Step 1: Assess. Write down a current or past situation in which you were in conflict.

_____

_____

_____

_____

_____

How did you respond internally? (Fast heartbeat, sweaty palms, dry mouth?)

_____

_____

_____

_____

_____

How did you respond externally? (Did you yell, get an attitude, shut down?)

_____

_____

_____

_____

_____

_____

_____

How did the other person respond? Describe their body gestures.

_____

_____

_____

_____

_____

_____

Step 2: Analyze. Determine why you are or were feeling stressed in this situation. What has occurred that has caused you to feel stressed? For example:

Why is the other person acting rude or abrasive toward you?

_____

_____

_____

_____

_____

What situation has occurred that has caused you both to be stressed? (Is there an immediate deadline, are you behind schedule on an assignment, are you overwhelmed with too many assignments, do you have a problem with the person you are in conflict with? If so what is that issue, specifically?)

_____

_____

_____

_____

_____

Why do you believe the other person is stressed? Are they behind schedule on work assignments, are they overwhelmed?

_____

_____

_____

_____

_____

_____

Step 3: Act. Once you have carefully assessed and analyzed the situation, you can respond most appropriately.

Think about how you responded initially. Was it an impulsive response or a kneejerk reaction? Or was it measured and thoughtful?

_____

_____

_____

_____

_____

If you could respond differently now that you have assessed and analyzed, how would you respond?

Before assessing and analyzing

_____

_____

_____

How I originally responded ...

_____

_____

_____

After assessing and analyzing

_____

_____

_____

How I should have responded ...

_____

_____

_____

7

FIVE STAR TRAITS

Whether you are a Millennial searching for your dream job, or
a Baby Boomer searching for a paid or volunteer opportunity after
retirement, or for any other generation in the workforce, you will
need the ability to interact and communicate effectively with other
people, including jerks (such as the people you consider to have
tough personalities and behaviors) to get things done. You will need
a flexible set of skills that will help you diffuse tense situations and
alleviate stress when dealing with others, especially with the people
you can't stand.

Additionally, employers will need to create an atmosphere where
employees feel valued, appreciated and engaged in order to retain
those employees and get maximum productivity out of them.
If employers fail to do this, companies can anticipate constant
employee turnover, low morale and workplace instability. This type
of inconsistency creates a problem for employers when it comes to
retaining top talent. It translates into sunk costs in wasted resources
spent on training and onboarding them into the job.

How can we address these issues affecting the workforce? How can
employers retain talented employees and avoid the wasted costs
associated with training and investing in new people who might just
flee? How do employees acquire the tools needed to get work done

with the people they can't stand? What tools can they use to handle stressful and challenging situations professionally and thoroughly?

In addition to the AAA method, you will need to use what I call the Five Star Traits when dealing with coworkers and management staff — whether they are a jerk or possess "jerkish" qualities, or whether you have difficulty getting along with people in the workplace.

The work environment is more diverse than ever. There are multiple generations in the workforce who represent people of different cultures, religion, and ethnicity. We have been introduced to new ways of interacting with others and getting our work done. Considering today's ever-changing environment, I have come up with the following traits that accurately reflect what we need in order to improve production and work better with our colleagues. These traits are: **Recognition, Poise, Drive, Perspective, and Rapport.**

★ Recognition
★ Poise
★ Perspective
★ Drive
★ Rapport

Examining each of these traits will allow you to understand their importance in the workplace and how to apply them. You may discover that you may have already made good use of at least one of these traits at times throughout your life.

> Success depends on your ability to stay composed in adversity, manage conflict and manage relationships.

These traits fall under these three aspects and will be introduced according to each category.

- *Composure*
  Composing yourself most appropriately and professionally when interacting with others in stressful situations. **Recognition and Drive fall into this category.**

- *Managing Conflict*
  The ability to diffuse tense situations, resolve disagreements, address problems with others. **Poise falls into this category.**

- *Managing Relationships*
  The ability to work with others productively and respectfully, especially people who have different personalities. **Perspective and Rapport fall into this category.**

RECOGNITION

| *Keep your head on a swivel ...*

Have you ever felt a particular way and didn't know why? Recognition is the ability to know what you are feeling and why, such as recognizing and understanding your personal moods, emotions and drives, as well as your effect on others.

In this chapter, you will learn how recognition:

- Benefits employees' ability to compose themselves in tough situations

- Helps business leaders' ability to initiate change, and

- Aids entrepreneurs in making the right business decisions.

Recognition depends on your ability to monitor your own emotional state and to correctly recognize your emotions. It also requires the ability to understand your surroundings and the situations or incidents that may trigger specific types of emotions and behaviors. I also refer to recognition as "keeping your head on a swivel," meaning you must be alert and aware of what your behavior is signaling to others and how it may be interpreted during particular situations — especially in confrontations or conflicts.

For example, about a year ago I delivered a keynote speech on leadership for a company that was promoting career development. One of the key takeaways from the speech was that you don't have to be in a leadership position (such as supervisor or manager) in order to be an effective leader. Among the many employees who approached me after the speech was one person who still stands out in memory. She told me that during her recent performance discussion, her boss mentioned that she needs to have a more positive attitude. He said that, at times, she appears frustrated when receiving a new work assignment. He observed that she rolls her eyes, sighs, or is sometimes non responsive. He told her that she comes off as if she has a bad attitude and that she does not want to do her work and that she seems unapproachable.

She told me that she did not understand why he would think that. She was completely unaware of how she was responding in those situations. She admitted to me that she was frustrated when doing the work, but she thought nobody noticed because she thought she did a good job of hiding her frustration.

I asked her a very important question. This question is key to recognizing your behavior in these types of situation. I asked her why she was frustrated. She explained that she receives little direction from her boss when she receives an assignment and each time she would submit the assignment, he would change his mind and direct her to do it a different way. She felt it was a waste of time because he does not provide clear direction and can never make up his mind on what he needed done. She said that if she had a different boss who was more decisive and gave clearer directions, she would not be so frustrated.

Unfortunately, most of us don't have the luxury of choosing our boss. We have to manage the situation as best as we can to get through those tough situations. I am sure that many of you may share this woman's frustration. I would be frustrated too when dealing with someone who cannot make up their mind and changes direction after you complete the assignment! When dealing with these types of situations where you are frustrated with a colleague or your boss, many times we unknowingly express our displeasure through our body language. We may suck our teeth, roll our eyes, or maybe shut down and not respond at all. When this happens, it sends a message to your audience about how you feel.

Even if you are having a bad day and your attitude is unrelated to the situation at work, it still sends a signal to your audience about your attitude and how you are feeling.

I told the employee it is good that she understands when she gets frustrated. That is the first step in recognizing your emotions and behavior before you can manage them most appropriately. I told her each time she gets frustrated and wants to roll her eyes or suck her teeth when her boss gives her a new assignment, she needs to take a moment to acknowledge the source of her frustration. The source of the frustration is the wasted time it takes to complete the assignment due to the lack of clear direction she receives from her boss.

So, what can she do to address that frustration? She can take proactive measures to ensure she not only understands the assignment, but also holds her boss accountable for delivering a clear message. She can do the following: I recommend you take similar action when you need to clarify additional work assignments.

How to Get Clarity from Your Boss on Additional Work Assignments

- Ask follow-up questions to get a better understanding of the assignment

- Determine where this assignment falls within the priority of other assignments you manage

- Schedule a meeting to get better context of the assignment and clarity on the expectations

- Provide a status update before the assignment is complete to make sure you are on the right track.

Interestingly, these same tips work if you're a consultant or service provider and are working with clients who tend to be unclear about expectations.

RECOGNIZING OUR EMOTIONS

On many occasions, perception is reality. People may perceive your bad attitude as proof that you're someone who is unapproachable and not a team player. By lacking recognition and being unaware of what your behavior is signaling to others, you may be continually surprised when people believe you are a jerk and will avoid working with you. In reality, you may be rightfully frustrated or may simply be having a bad day. The better we become at recognizing our emotions and how they may affect others, the less we become jerks because we are better positioned to manage our emotions in a more productive and professional way. This creates a better opportunity at controlling the outcome of the situation before it escalates.

For example, imagine you are having a bad day at work. Your work continues to pile up, your phone will not stop ringing, and your boss is upset about the direction of your projects. The only thing you want to do is go home because the slightest thing will tick you off. You receive a phone call from one of your colleagues complaining about one of your projects. That was the last straw! You behave like a jerk. Your response to your colleague is short, abrasive, sarcastic and definitely regrettable. Now you face the following consequences: your colleague may complain to your boss, your actions may have ruined your relationship with your colleague, you may face being reprimanded or other disciplinary actions by your boss, and you may have to apologize to both your boss and your colleague for your actions.

One Chance to Make a Good Impression

When situations like this occur, you will need to become aware of your emotions and how they are reflecting outwardly — *before* your respond to the situation. This will keep you from becoming a jerk, making a serious mistake that you will be unable to take back. In the work environment, most times, it only takes one time to act out of line before you become labeled as a jerk with a bad attitude or as someone who is difficult to get along with. This can stick with you throughout your career. It is well documented that people deserve and sometimes receive second chances, but people do not forget what you did and how you reacted like a jerk. If you are seeking a promotion or different assignment, your boss and colleagues may keep in mind how you reacted that one time when you were not recognizing your behavior and you reacted in a rude, abrasive manner.

RECOGNIZING WHAT YOU WANT

People who practice recognition become more responsible, professional and strategic. They are also better negotiators and often find solutions when there are problems. Recognizing your emotions not only helps you become a better employee and colleague, but it also builds your confidence to ask for what you want, such as a raise, a promotion or a reassignment. This helps all generations but particularly favors Millennials in the work environment because they are more likely to request promotions or ask to work some place they believe will make them happy. It is always encouraged to ask for what you want, but some people don't because they may be either too afraid, too shy or don't recognize the right way to approach their objective. You must ask for what you want in a tactful, professional way with serious thought.

When you have a desire to move on and do something new in your career, you can experience all types of emotions. Whether it's fear about telling your supervisor about your career aspirations or anger toward others who happen to get different career opportunities instead of you, it is important that you recognize those feelings before you plan your next move.

For example, one of my clients told me she was nervous about formally asking to leave her current job for another one she desired. She had just returned from doing an assignment in another location and was disappointed that she could not stay at that assignment permanently. She was unhappy about returning to her old job. She was upset and felt as if her director was purposely keeping her from being happy and doing a job that she enjoyed. She took it personally. That situation made it uneasy for her to have a conversation with her boss about wanting to leave.

She asked me for advice on how to deal with the situation. I asked her if she had had that conversation with her director previously. She replied "not formally", and that she may have eluded to her unhappiness. I told her that if she truly is unhappy, she should discuss with her immediate supervisor and inform him about her unhappiness and plans to discuss with her director. I told her it was okay to ask for what she wants, but there are ways to do it effectively and ineffectively. She has the right to voice her concerns in a professional manner. But it is also important for her to understand the situation and her emotions so that she can approach it the right way and get her desired result. I reminded her that there may be other employees who are unhappy as well. In addition, at some point, they too will want to voice their concerns. So what makes her different from the rest? How can she get what she wants if others who feel the same way confront their boss expressing the same unhappiness? It is more than likely that the boss will not allow her entire staff to leave, so the employee needs to approach this situation in a different manner to make herself stand out from the rest.

"What will make you different from the next person who confronts their boss to leave?" I asked her. She did not know. I recommended that she clearly articulate her goals and professional aspirations. This means documenting her career path and showing upper management that she is taking her career seriously and understands what she wants to do professionally. It means understanding and demonstrating how she can add value to the company. This also shows management that she is not just complaining or voicing a concern, but that she has a solution for her concerns and that she is showing initiative toward pursuing her goals.

> It's okay to be an employee with a problem; but it's always best to be an employee who has a solution to the problem too.

Asking for what you want in the workplace means taking time for careful planning and strategic thinking. You want to display professionalism, confidence and sincerity while controlling your emotions so that you can clearly articulate what you want. If you allow your emotions to cloud your judgment, you may forget the points that you intended to make, you may not appear to be as composed as you would like, or you may embarrass yourself and ruin any future chances of getting what you want. Depending on what it is that you want, you will need to take serious consideration of your approach because it may involve different people and it might be outside of one individual's control.

> *"To have greater self-awareness or understanding means to have a better grasp of reality." – Dalai Lama*

THE SEINFELD EFFECT

The *Seinfeld* sitcom was a big hit in the 1990s. To this day, it's one of my favorite television shows to watch. Although known for its comedy, it should also be known for demonstrating what happens when people fail to recognize their moods and behaviors when interacting with others in their personal and professional relationships. For example, the *Seinfeld* episode "The Revenge" provides a good explanation of what can happen when one fails to recognize the impact the situation has on his behavior, which leads to a regrettable outcome. In this episode, George Costanza storms into his boss's office, upset that he cannot use his boss's bathroom. He is so upset that he insults him and then declares, "I quit!" It wasn't until he told his friend Jerry Seinfeld about the situation that he realized he acted like a jerk, didn't have a plan B, and that he made a big mistake. He reacted on impulse. Jerry tried to convince him to return to work as if it never happened. Even if you have not watched this episode, I am sure you can imagine what happened — it was not well received!

The bottom line of this story is that if George had taken a moment to reflect on his emotions and recognize why he was upset, he most likely would have been more strategic and dealt with the situation in a better manner instead of acting like a jerk and making an impulsive decision to quit his job. He should have been more deliberate in recognizing his feelings and been more introspective by asking,

- "Why am I so upset?"
- "Why am I feeling this way?"
- Even more importantly, he could have asked himself, "Would it be wise to verbally react to what I'm feeling in this moment?"

We are reminded of these types of situations each day in the work environment. Many people can relate to making impulsive, irrational decisions. Even worse, many people have regretted actually making these decisions.

Understanding your emotions and being able to identify them is critical to your success and your ability to properly approach tough situations rather than responding like a jerk.

RECOGNITION FOR LEADERSHIP

Recognizing your emotions is just as important for employees as it is for managers, supervisors and other leaders because it can mean the difference between staying employed or losing your job (or your sanity).

Recognition not only helps you handle day-to-day situations in your current job, it also helps leaders implement change effectively. An executive in the public sector once told me that recognizing your emotions and behaviors is one of the most important leadership qualities all employees must possess — especially Millennials. She says that it is important to do a health check and assess situations. Recognizing how your actions and behaviors affect others and how external surroundings affect you is key to helping you manage your behavior in a professional way. She added that recognizing your emotions helps you make better decisions because you are allowing yourself to better understand yourself and others with clarity. She also says that as a leader, recognizing not only *your* emotions and behaviors but the emotions and behaviors of *others* helps you become strategic in determining the next course of action. I could not agree more.

Let me share an example from this very executive's organization. She had recently led efforts to reorganize her division of the company. In this situation, the reorganization involved two departments merging to form one department. The change would impact hundreds of employees. As a result of this reorganization, there would be several changes. There were leadership changes, employees' responsibilities changed, and the work culture changed. Knowing that she had been involved in several types of reorganization efforts in the past, she recognized that it would weaken morale if she did not effectively communicate the reorganization activities with her staff and explain the reasons that prompted the reorganization. During prior reorganizations, the employees knew little about the reasons for it and had little input before, during or after the process. As a result, the employees resented management, some left for a different place to work and, for the most part, morale was low. For a very long time, that resentment of leadership lingered and employed lacked trust in the people they reported to because when stakes had been high, leaders had acted like jerks.

This time around, the executive's use of recognition helped her avoid some of the pitfalls she encountered before. Recognizing that she may have been overconfident the last time around based on how her staff responded after the previous reorganization, it gave her some pause about moving forward in the same manner. This time, she paid attention to her staff's emotional reaction to the reorganization before implementing it. On the office floor, she saw people concerned, and worried about what the change would mean to them. She observed others rolling their eyes and sucking their teeth in frustration, blaming her for the change. She began to listen to their concerns and got their feedback about the situation. She realized that they needed to understand what prompted the reorganization and the impact it would have on them so they can understand the full picture. Without that understanding, her staff would continue to blame her and perceive her as making a unilateral decision to suit her own needs. She worked hard to make this most recent reorganization transparent and she involved the staff in the process, from beginning to end.

WHAT EXACTLY DID SHE DO?

- She received input from the staff and suggestions for implementing the reorganization
- She explained the reason for the reorganization and
- She allowed her employees to play an active role in the process.

This example underscores the importance of leaders recognizing situations in the work environment and how their emotions and behaviors play a role in the outcome of those situations. If this executive did not take the time to recognize the situation and learn from her past mistakes, she may not have effectively executed the reorganization process and her employees would have perceived her acting like a jerk. This required a level of tact and strategic thinking to implement the reorganization, but it also required her to be aware of the impact this would have on hundreds of employees. In the end, she realized that she needed their buy-in and support in order to merge the two divisions effectively. Her approach to the situation enabled great results.

HOW RECOGNITION HELPS ENTREPRENEURS

Recognizing your emotions is equally important for entrepreneurs — especially for two or more people who decide to go into business together. According to the *Entrepreneur* article titled "How Important is Emotional Intelligence to Success in Business?," successful entrepreneurs are able to understand what is going on in their own heads and what is driving their emotions. They are able to understand what makes them angry, happy or sad. In order to be successful you have to understand yourself. This may sound easy, but for many people it is rather difficult.

For example, ever since I started my own business as a professional speaker, I encountered many other successful entrepreneurs who told me that starting your own business is hard work. I will admit that I didn't fully grasp this because I was so sure of myself and passionate about helping and inspiring others. Little did I know that it takes much more than passion and confidence to start a business. I felt frustrated, annoyed and bitter when I couldn't land any paid speaking gigs after the first year. I felt defeated and wanted to quit. It wasn't until late that I learned that most businesses fail after only a few years in business. I soon realized that I wasn't the only one in this situation. I was surprised to learn that some entrepreneurs were worse off than me!

It validated what other successful entrepreneurs said about starting your own business being hard work. I learned that starting your own business is not just about doing your passion. It's so much more than that! Even if you're a one-person operation, you have to *run* your business like a CEO runs a company of any size and in any industry. You must learn how to market your company, network with others, learn about financial accounting and so much more! Most of all, I learned you have to be honest with yourself and understand who you are and who you want to be. Steve Jobs, Jeff Bezos and Bill Gates didn't become successful overnight. They failed plenty of times and faced countless rejections. What made them different? They practiced recognition! Their feelings of frustration reminded them of their purpose and why they wanted to start their businesses in the first place. Being aware of their feelings motivated them to push further in spite of failure and rejection.

I realized that each time I sulked and felt depressed when I failed to get a speaking gig, I was unmotivated and stopped moving forward; this hurt my business even more. But when I practiced recognition,

I became aware of these feelings and how it stunted my growth. It forced me to come to terms with what I really wanted out of this business and how far I was willing to go to be successful. Instead of sulking and feeling depressed and defeated every time I failed to get a speaking gig, I practiced recognition and confronted my emotions and realized that feeling down and defeated when rejected wasn't helping me one bit. Those were emotional traps that kept me from moving forward. I turned those feelings into a burning desire to never give up. That burning desire motivated me to keep moving forward to find things that work, such as getting a mentor. I am committed to this for the long haul!

For entrepreneurs who continue to feel frustrated and defeated after facing rejection and failure countless times, here is how you can use recognition to turn things around and get you out of your funk.

- **Assess.** Understand why you are feeling frustrated. It may be much more than feeling frustrated over rejection. You may realize you're frustrated because you are in it for the wrong reasons. You might even discover that, in the end, you're unwilling to go the extra mile to improve your business.

- **Analyze.** Determine what situations make you feel this way. For example, perhaps you have plenty of clients but not enough people to support you and run the day-to-day operations. This can be overwhelming.

- **Act.** Once you understand why you are frustrated and what causes your frustration, you can act most accordingly. In this situation, I would recommend you find an experienced mentor who can provide insight and guidance on your issue.

IT'S BUSINESS, NOT PERSONAL

When I collaborated with two others to form a business, it took me some time to understand why I was so frustrated with working with them after only a few months. The business was a three-leader partnership between myself, a previous colleague and that colleague's father. Even though all three of us were business partners, it is important to note that the other two business partners were father and daughter. This would make things very difficult as the business progressed, because our personal and professional business relationship changed. This affected our business relationship in the beginning because the two other partners had a very close relationship, thus creating a difference in our views about the direction of the business. They sided with one another in every decision matter. It was stressful for me because my opinions were not valued as much in the partnership; they shut me out of the decision-making. When I offered suggestions about a different approach, they dismissed it.

In their minds, they had their own ideas about their vision for the business and how to run it. To keep a professional working relationship, and to understand why I was feeling so strained, I had to recognize my feelings and why I was so frustrated. I really wanted the business to be successful, but if I allowed my frustration to get the best of me, I would have said some hurtful, regrettable things. After countless discussions with my family about my unhappiness with how I was being treated, I decided that the best thing to do to alleviate my tension and frustration, and regain my sanity was to dissolve my stake in the partnership. I did not make this decision overnight. I had to take a moment to reflect on my feelings before making a decision. By recognizing my feelings, and realizing why I was stressed and frustrated, I was able to carefully consider the pros and cons to this decision.

At first, I felt conflicted because I was really committed to the business venture and wanted it to succeed. I thought it would offer a lot of value to people who wanted to improve their personal lives and professional careers. But, once I realized that continuing to work with the two partners meant I would never really have the opportunity to offer that value I had dreamed of, I knew I would be doing myself and my family a disservice by continuing along this path. I would have dedicated all my time to pursuing *their* personal interests instead of what we agreed to when I first went into business with them. Therefore, I dissolved my stake in the partnership, clear about why I was doing what I was doing, and confident I was making the right choice.

Had I not recognized my feelings and been aware of the situation, I could have made some erratic, impulsive decisions. I could have remained an unhappy business partner, but that would result in me becoming a jerk, engaging in more conflict, combative behavior, and more problems among us. It would have resulted in more stress for my family, my business partners and myself. It also would have taken away from my already successful business, Tailored Training Solutions, which was a driving reason why it was important for me to dissolve my partnership amicably to avoid any ill will and focus on my own business. I wanted to maintain my professionalism. Since then, I have not regretted my decision. In fact, I have been stress-free and have been able to focus my efforts on growing my business. Now I have an opportunity and the freedom to do the things they did not want to do in their business. I found that it was possible to wish them every luck in the world, and still step away to pursue business on my own terms.

FIVE-STEP PROCESS FOR RESOLVING CONFLICT WITH BUSINESS PARTNERS

Upon realizing I was not happy or being treated well in my former business venture, I employed the following process to deal with the situation appropriately instead of rushing to judgment and ultimately acting like a jerk. Although you may not have shared my experience, these steps — or some customized variation of them — will help you take a more thoughtful, pragmatic approach when dealing with conflict with your business partners or other vital collaborators.

I recognized my emotions and my behavior. After every business meeting or conference call with the other two partners, I would feel annoyed and frustrated. I only came to terms with those feelings once I realized that I was happy and generally in a good mood *before* meeting with them. I identified the root cause of my frustrations by determining why I was upset and what was causing me to be upset. I realized I was upset because my opinions and feedback on the direction of the business were being dismissed.

I solicited feedback from my wife. She observed my frustrations and sensed that I was stressed often, especially after the business meetings.

I wrote down my frustrations. I jotted down my jerkish thoughts and feelings about why I felt so frustrated while working with those business partners. I compared those feelings to how I felt when I first went into business with them. I also compared those feelings to how I feel when I work on my own personal business. The difference was obvious. It was like night and day. When I first went into business with them, I felt excited and inspired because I would be helping others improve their lives and accomplish their goals. That feeling soon changed when I realized they wanted to move the business in a different direction and my ideas for moving the business forward were quickly dismissed without any explanation. Instead of working together to carry out the intended mission of the business, I realized I was helping my business partners pursue their personal agenda. I realized that I did not have a place in the business and I was unhappy because I was taking meaningful time away from my own business to help them.

I dissolved my stake in the business amicably. I knew I wanted out of the business, but I did not know how to get out. I wanted to keep my emotions in check. Before we went into business together, we were good friends. We talked frequently and went to lunch often. I had to separate the personal relationship from the business relationship. I made sure my decision was simply and purely a decision based on differing ideas of the direction of the business.

I drafted a dissolution agreement to move forward with exiting the business. Although we were friends before going into business, I wanted to end it in the right way and protect myself from any legal issues that may arise in the future.

By understanding the situation, I could make these decisions carefully and with clarity. Reflecting on the situation, getting my wife's feedback, and jotting down my thoughts and feelings kept me from making an emotional, impulsive decision. To this day, I am proud of this decision and have no regrets.

Whether it's maintaining good relationships with our coworkers, advancing our careers, or simply avoiding unnecessary conflict, we must be able to recognize our emotions and how they affect others in the workplace. Our happiness and success depend upon it.

RECOGNIZING YOUR EMOTIONS

ACTIVITY 1

How can you practice recognizing your emotions? Follow these steps below:

- **Ask for informal feedback.** It's not always easy to invite people to give you feedback. It takes courage and ignoring your ego. *Do not let your ego become your amigo!* Allow others to give you feedback so you can improve. It always helps to get objective feedback from others.

- **Think on a regular basis.** Set aside some time where you can think about the day ahead or reflect on the day that passed in a quiet, uninterrupted place. Some people prefer to do this while meditating or doing yoga, while others enjoy peace and quiet. Whatever you prefer, it is helpful for you to think privately on a regular basis about whatever you are dealing with. This kind of self-introspection helps you think clearly and calmly and plan appropriately.

- **Write in a journal**. Sometimes it is helpful to put your thoughts or feelings down on paper to draw clarity from situations. It also helps you easily identify your feelings when you encounter similar situations, allowing you to respond better in the future.

- **Take a personality test.** I recommend using the Myers-Briggs and the DiSC Assessment personality tests. They are popular, highly reputable personality tests and are available for free online. Check out www.16Personalities.com to take a free personality test. This is often done in certain work environments. There are many different types of personality tests and I have taken a few throughout my career. I always learn something new, but some of the most interesting things I have learned are (1) How my personality and behavior has evolved since the first time I took the test with each new and significant experience, and (2) How to better understand other people's personalities. Learning about others helps me understand myself better, and flex my work style to accommodate others in a non-jerkish way.

ACTIVITY 2

The best way to recognize your emotions is to practice. This means, intentionally and immediately identifying your emotions and behaviors, and being able to recognize the situation.

To clearly identify, articulate, and understand your emotions and behaviors, visit my website at www.TailoredTrainingSolutions.com to get a free chart that lists possible emotions or behaviors you may possibly experience.

Below is an exercise that will help you practice understanding your emotions based on situations. Provide the response to your emotions to help you identify your triggers. The quicker you identify your triggers, the better you can control the outcome of your message or situation. Review the examples before trying it on your own.

Examples

- **Situation:** I get upset when people are rude to me.
  Physical response: When I am upset, my heart beats very fast, my mouth gets dry, and I shut down and ignore others.

- **Situation:** I get frustrated because my colleagues don't appear to value my opinion.
  Physical response: When I am frustrated, I start to sweat, and I have an attitude and I am negative.

- **Situation:** I get sad because I have not achieved my goals.
  Physical response: When I am sad, I feel depressed and avoid people.

Now it's your turn!

1. **Situation:**

   I get upset when _____

   _____

   Physical response:

   When I am upset, _____

   _____

2. **Situation:**

I get frustrated because _____

_____

Physical response:

When I am frustrated, _____

_____

3. **Situation:**

I get sad because _____

_____

Physical response:

When I am sad, _____

_____

POISE

> *"Life is ten percent what happens to you and ninety percent how you respond to it."* – Lou Holtz

Recognition may be the tool that helps you identify how your emotions and behaviors are being perceived outwardly, but poise is the tool that will help you manage your emotions or behavior to prevent you from responding like a jerk, especially when dealing with conflict.

In this chapter, you will learn how poise:

- Benefits employees' ability to resolve differences with colleagues and advance their careers

- Prevents business leaders from creating toxic work environments, and

- Aids entrepreneurs in making the right business decisions.

Poise is a necessary trait to have in today's professional environment and in your personal life. It allows you to keep a cool head in stressful situations and prevents you from making kneejerk reactions or impulsive responses. Quite simply, poise is a tool that helps you think before you act like a jerk. Employees, supervisors and business leaders must demonstrate poise when interacting with others during conflict. Countless times, I have heard from people during my workshops or after my keynote speeches who have regretted the outcome of situations, or made bad situations worse due to making a rash decision without demonstrating poise and taking the time to think things through.

POISE FOR EMPLOYEES

I delivered a keynote speech on career development to an organization that employs more than 300 employees. After the keynote, I led a Q&A session addressing how to overcome some of the obstacles we may encounter when trying to advance our careers. One of the employees described his difficulty getting along with another colleague on a joint project. He said that, at times, he has difficulty coming to an agreement with another colleague on a particular direction of a project. Several years and millions of dollars have already been invested in this project. He did not feel confident in the direction of the project and recommended to delay the project's implementation so they can have enough time to address some serious concerns that will have a direct impact on the customers. His colleague, on the other hand, who has worked on this project since its inception, wants to move forward with the implementation, stating it's a minor issue that can be addressed quickly.

He described how they had heated discussions about the project and he let his emotions get the best of him, blurting out some personal and hurtful things toward his colleague. He responded like a jerk because he did not think before he acted. His reason for lashing out that day was a culmination of things that transpired that day. He was having a difficult day at work. Nothing was going his way. He began the day stuck in traffic. When he arrived to work, his boss was concerned about the status of the project and was demanding updates. Meanwhile, he had other work assignments that required his attention.

"IT'S ALL YOUR FAULT!"

His phone kept ringing all day. Finally, his colleague who is working on the project with him stopped by his cubicle to discuss the direction of the project and what to say to their boss. That was the spark that set him off. Instead of taking a moment to take a breath and collect his thoughts, he blurted out the first thing that entered his mind and told his coworker he was acting like a jerk and was incapable of handling the project and blamed him for the problems.

The argument quickly turned into a shouting match for everyone to see and hear — especially his boss.

He told me that he regretted that the situation occurred because it put him in a bad light and he feels it has hurt his attempts for a promotion. I told him that, unfortunately, these incidents are quite common. Sometimes we find ourselves in a situation where we avoid addressing the situation as soon as it occurs, allowing stress to take its toll, keeping things inside until we reach a boiling point, or are caught up in the heat of the moment, and we do things we regret. Luckily, there are steps we can take to manage conflict more professionally and productively.

This brings us back to the aforementioned AAA method that I described earlier in the book: Assess, Analyze, Act. During the Q&A session, I recommended he take the following steps when dealing with conflict.

Step 1: Assess the situation. When dealing with conflict at work or in your personal life, it is important to assess the situation. This involves not only being aware of your emotions and how you are feeling, but how the other person is feeling too. Reflect on a specific situation you have experienced to identify these emotions. What does your behavior or body language signal to the other person? What behavior or body language is that person signaling to you? Sometimes when we are stressed or dealing with a difficult situation, we can exhibit at least one or more of the following reactions. Our heart may beat fast, we can get shortness of breath, we may clinch up or feel our palms getting sweaty.

Not only should you be aware of your body gestures and other's body gestures, you should also be aware of the current situation or the circumstance. For example, are you stressed because you have an immediate deadline you are struggling to meet? Are there multiple things going on at the same time that may be overwhelming and you may be unsure what priority to tackle first?

Find the Root Cause of Your Frustrations

In the situation described above, in which two project collabora-tors blew up within ear-shot of the boss, the gentleman who shared his story with me needed to assess the root cause of his frustrations when working on the project. He was frustrated because the project was going in the wrong direction and he could not get his coworker to understand why they needed to delay it to iron out the issues before moving forward.

Step 2: Analyze the situation. Once you have assessed the situation and are aware of what your emotions and behaviors are signaling to others, the next step is to analyze your emotions and behaviors. Determine why you are feeling stressed. What situation has occurred that has caused you to feel stressed? Additionally, seek to understand and reflect on the thoughts and feelings of the other person involved. Why is the other person acting rude or abrasive toward you? What situation has occurred that has caused you both to be stressed?

In the employee's situation, he needs to seek to understand his colleague's point of view. His colleague has more experience and has been working on the project much longer than he has. Why does his colleague believe the issue is so minor? Why isn't he as concerned? Perhaps there was merit to his confidence in moving forward.

Step 3: Act. Once you have a full understanding of the situation — meaning you are aware of what has caused you or the other person to be stressed and you understand what may be contributing to these feelings — you can respond and act most appropriately instead of lashing out like a jerk. This is one of the most important steps because it prevents you from allowing your emotions to get the best of you and keeps you from making an impulsive decision you will most likely regret.

Bottom line is that the employee in this situation should have a heart-to-heart with the colleague. It's not too late to meet with the colleague to not only understand his perspective but to share his own. This approach involves both people working together to get on the same page and determine how best to move forward. It also allows both the opportunity to voice any concerns or explain the reasons for having different opinions. This allows him and his colleague to have a unified message when briefing management and other stakeholders.

I mentioned to this keynote audience that employees who lack poise are the same people who can respond like a jerk because they are unable to control their emotions. And failure to control our emotions during high-stakes work will have a direct impact on getting our ability to get work done. As a former employee, I can relate to this because I have spent several hours dealing with conflict rather than focusing on my own work. Or I have been at odds with someone who I needed information from. I avoided them as often as possible, which made it harder for me to get work done.

When employees allow their emotions to get the best of them, they risk jeopardizing their job, damaging relationships with their coworkers and boss, and ruin the quality of their work because they are caught up in the heat of the moment.

There's no escaping the fact that it's extremely difficult for employees to control their emotions while in the heat of an argument. Under high stress, employees' ability to control their emotions and remain poised takes a back seat. But hard as it can be, employees must demonstrate poise, take a measured approach when dealing with conflict to get work done and find productive ways to work with their colleagues.

POISE FOR LEADERS

"If I can just get rid of her, everything will eventually be fine."

It is especially important for leaders to demonstrate poise when interacting with their staff. That's because they are responsible with leading and inspiring others to get work done. If leaders fail to have poise, not only can they act like jerks, they can create toxic work environments, low morale and disengaged staff.

In an article by Amy Castro, "Does Your Next Generation of Leaders Possess These Critical Communication Skills?," we learn that the next generation of leaders must not only understand their emotions and how it impacts others, but must demonstrate poise in order to lead their staff. In public sector organizations, she has seen all kinds of bad behavior in leaders when it comes to expressing their feelings: employees buried under a mountain of profanity, sarcastic leaders who belittle others, and the opposite extreme — leaders who are too weak to express the seriousness of a situation and how they feel about it. Castro says that leaders who act out their emotions are destined to fail.

When leaders allow their emotions to get the best of them, they can lash out at their staff, acting like a jerk, and end up regretting it because they were caught up in the moment. Leaders can end up in serious trouble when this happens. For example, leaders who lack poise, react on impulse and fail to control their emotions can:

- Face unnecessary grievances
- Become subject to equal employment opportunity complaints, or even worse,
- Lose their leadership position.

This could have very well happened to a supervisor in the story I describe below. Although he made a bad decision, he was willing to take the necessary steps to turn things around.

A few months ago, I conducted a workshop with a group of supervisors about how to get maximum performance out of their staff.
Some shared their frustrations about their staff and their challenges
of getting them to perform. One manager talked about his staff's lack
of engagement and about how his direct reports hardly speak to him
unless when absolutely necessary — appearing as if they are trying to
avoid him. He believed that it was one particular employee who was
to blame. He described her as not only performing poorly, but also
having a bad attitude and influence over others, who she encouraged
to distance themselves from him. She acted like a jerk. He believed
she was to blame for the entire team's lack of engagement and
low morale.

He said, "If I can just get rid of her, everything will eventually be fine."
He explained how he would get frustrated every time he stopped by
her desk to follow up on a work assignment and she had an excuse
about why she didn't get it done. He felt she was purposely challenging his authority to prove a point to the rest of the staff. One day
during a staff meeting, he asked her for a status on a project and she
explained that she didn't have time to work on it. The manager told
me that he lost his cool. He acted like a jerk, scolding her during the
meeting in front of the rest of the staff about not completing her work
assignments, accusing her of trying to sabotage the office production, before finally dismissing her from the meeting. He said that the
rest of the team appeared to be in shock and that it was a good thing
because it would send a message to the rest of the team that such
behavior is unacceptable.

This was a good opportunity for me to discuss the concept of poise
and to help him understand how his behavior may have affected the
team and could be contributing to a toxic work environment with
low morale and limited employee engagement. I explained that his

reaction, although meant to warn others to be prepared for meetings, could have had the opposite effect on his staff. **Leaders should not manage others through intimidation, fear or threats.** Those are jerkish qualities and the wrong way to get the attention of people you're trying to lead, support and inspire.

No matter how stressful things get, staff need to see their leaders maintain a level head and stay in control. If they see their leaders lose control and lash out at their staff, they will be afraid to approach their boss or be engaged in the workplace. They may even resent their boss. This makes a bad situation worse, keeping the morale low and productivity down.

I worked with him during a one-on-one session to come up with some alternative ways to respond in a more controlled manner, demonstrating poise, while still achieving his ultimate goal — to correct the employee's behavior who was giving him a hard time. Earlier he stated that if he could get rid of her, he wouldn't have those problems. But that is just a temporary solution — a bandage for a wound that needs proper treatment. I encouraged him to deal with the conflict at hand instead of avoiding it or lashing out. I recommended the AAA Method, which is similar to the situation above only it is more tailored to suit the supervisor's needs.

Step 1: Assess the situation. The supervisor had to assess the root cause of his frustrations when dealing with the employee. He was

frustrated that she was not completing her assigned tasks. He thought she was challenging his authority and creating a toxic environment and encouraging others to act out.

Step 2: Analyze the problem you want solved. At first, this was a little bit unclear. Initially, it appeared that he wanted his staff to respect him. But after further discussion, we drilled down to something more specific. We determined that he wanted his employee to complete his staff assignments, especially since he did not have this problem with others. The supervisor had to seek to understand and reflect on the employee's point of view. Is the employee dealing with a personal problem that's keeping her from doing her assigned tasks? Is it a performance problem? Conduct problem? Lack of communication? Does she really have more on her plate than he realized?

Step 3: Act. He needed to have a discussion with the employee. He met with the employee to not only apologize for lashing out, but to also understand her perspective and to share his perspective and also to set clear expectations when making assignments and determine how they can support each other to ensure those expectations are met. This approach involves the employee in the process for resolving the issue. It also allows the employee the opportunity to voice any concerns or explain her reasons for not completing her work assignments. More importantly, it is a one-on-one discussion that does not involve the rest of the staff and does not embarrass anyone. The employee and the supervisor can get on the same page and can work together to resolve the conflict.

LESSONS LEARNED

After following these steps, the supervisor realized that his initial approach was over the top. He was a jerk when he lashed out because he wanted to prove a point to his staff that he should be respected. It had the opposite effect because people resented him and avoided him even more than before. It also showed his staff that he is not in control. Once he revisited the situation with the employee and followed the steps above, he had a much better outcome. Not only did he learn that she was dealing with an overwhelming personal matter, they worked together and came up with a plan to ensure she completed her work assignments on time, while ensuring account-ability and meeting expectations. More importantly, they gained a mutual respect for one another and found a better way to resolve their conflict.

As a manager, dealing with conflict with another employee in front of the staff requires poise to handle in the most appropriate and professional manner. You must be the steady hand and think carefully about how to resolve the conflict because you must set an example for how to act when dealing with conflict in the workplace. Allowing your emotions to get the best of you will keep you from making an informed decision and can make a bad situation worse.

Leaders who demonstrate poise are more successful than those who are unable to do so. They are more likely to advance their careers or receive raises or all the other perks that come with confidence and trust. They are more productive because they are able to focus more time and energy on getting the job done rather than arguing with others.

Leaders with poise are in high demand in organizations because they are able to control their behavior and maintain professionalism in tough situations. Leaders who demonstrate poise are able to work with all types of employees and manage the behavior and workplace results of entire teams.

USING POISE TO PROMOTE GOOD MORALE

Leaders in the workplace who demonstrate poise help promote employee morale. This is because they thoughtfully and professionally take their time to deliver a response, instead of responding on impulse. Employees appreciate this approach because it not only helps resolve conflict, but it also prevents unnecessary conflict, resentment, and hard feelings. These actions directly lead to improved productivity and help staff become more engaged in work activities, causing employees to remain at the place of employment. Employees choose to stay at a place where their employers value and respect them.

POISE FOR ENTREPRENEURS

It comes as no surprise that lack of poise does not bode well for entrepreneurs and business owners. I delivered a keynote speech at a summit for small business owners in Maryland and talked about the necessity for having poise. For entrepreneurs, success as a business owner depends on your ability to remain calm and poised during stressful situations. Entrepreneurs must interact with different people while addressing various issues regarding their business. No matter how big the problem is, you must manage your emotions accordingly. Clients and colleagues rely on a steady hand in order to do business. When faced with adversity or when having a bad day, it is important to stay poised and focused on the business and make sure that the customer is getting exactly the kind of service they expect and deserve to receive. Allowing your emotions to get the best of you will hurt your business's bottom line. And, you guessed it, you're apt to become a jerk along the way. At the end of the day, if you're a business owner, how you respond to conflict will have a trickledown effect that extends beyond your business to your family and friends who rely on you to support them.

Demonstrating poise in stressful situations can be difficult; however, it is not impossible. People who have been effective with controlling their emotions also understand their emotions before a complex situation can come to a head. They are aware of their feelings, emotions and behavior. Once they recognize these things, they can stop themselves from reacting on impulse. Instead of responding to that nasty email from their colleague, client or peer, they delay their response, remain poised and focus on the proper way to respond. These people have an understanding of things they can control and things they cannot. They understand that acting erratic, and being frustrated and angry is pointless because it will not help them resolve the issue. It only makes them look like the jerk they are surely becoming. Entrepreneurs with poise understand that the best way to resolve an issue is to practice the AAA Method: Assess, Analyze, and Act. This method, as you are learning, allows you to regroup, get the emotions under control and focus on how to solve the issue. All generations in the workplace can benefit from being poised in stressful situations because it will give them confidence to communicate more effectively with one another and resolve conflict with all types of people — especially with people we can't stand.

ACTIVITY 1

How can you exercise poise and avoid making impulsive decisions? Practice the AAA Method using a conflict situation you are dealing with now or have dealt with recently:

- **Assess.** Before making a decision, consider all the facts, take in all possible outcomes. Think about a situation where you were involved in conflict. How were you feeling? How did you behave? How did the other person (s) involved in the conflict respond?

- **Analyze.** Weigh decisions with care. What decisions are you considering or did you have to consider to resolve the conflict?

- **Act.** Don't respond immediately, take a moment, clear your head and relax. Avoid making decisions based on mood or feeling. How did you respond to the conflict? Did you take a moment to think things through or did you respond impulsively? What was the outcome? When determining how to respond when resolving conflict, consider creating a list and determining possible solutions. For example, below is a list you can create to help you determine the most appropriate way to act when resolving conflict.

Visit www.TailoredTrainingSolutions.com to get a free copy of your own template to jot down your possible actions to resolve conflict.

How to Respond to Conflict	Successful (Y/N)
Ignore the situation	
Tell the person how you feel	
Wait until the next day before responding	
Poke them between the eyes	
Get management help to resolve situation	

Use the steps you just reviewed and employ them in these
role-playing games with you and a partner:

1. **Managing Emotions**

You just purchased a brand-new luxury car! You take it for a spin to
show it off to your friends and family. While crossing a major inter-
section, you get into a car accident. Luckily, nobody is badly hurt, but
your new car is completely wrecked. Words cannot express how upset
you are. You believe the other person is at fault. Meanwhile, the other
driver gets out of the car and blames you. The both of you are highly
emotional and meet face-to-face, both believing that the accident is
the other person's fault. What do you do?

2. **Decision Making**

Congratulations! You and two of your friends or colleagues won
tickets to attend a concert of your favorite artist, and the concert is
in Jamaica. Unfortunately, you only have two first-class tickets. This
means that two of you will ride the plane first class while one of you
sits alone in coach. If you fly first class, you will be sitting with several
famous musicians and actors and you will have fun activities planned
during your flight, including top-notch meals and movies. If you fly
coach ... well, you know what that means. Who rides first class? How
do you decide who doesn't? How do you explain your rationale?

3. **Decision Making Under Stressful Circumstances**

As you are flying to Jamaica, the plane suffers severe turbulence and
goes DOWN! As the plane crashes, you discover you three, along
with a handful of little kids, are the only remaining survivors! It will
take several days for you to be rescued. You have a limited supply
of food and water. In order to survive until help comes, you have to

find shelter and food. The two people who decided to fly first class are badly injured and cannot walk. The kids are scared. You flew coach and only have minor bruises. Because you are the only healthy person, you have to make the decisions for survival. What do you do? Do you abandon your friends to find shelter? Do you find food? How do you ease the situation?

4. **Negotiating**

You are working on a proposal for a brand-new client to present in the morning but your neighbor is playing loud music, making it hard to concentrate. You need to do well on this proposal to expand your business. What do you do?

Note: The neighbor playing loud music is practicing for an audition the next day. If she does well at the audition, she gets to perform at a major event. Performing at this event will earn her recognition and money that she definitely needs.

Note: If the proposal goes well, you stand to sign an important new piece of business and earn a $10,000 bonus.

Poise Tips or Conflict

-   **Stay in control, calmly.** If you can control your response and channel your anger into an advantage, you are guaranteed to have a better outcome no matter who started it.

-   **Don't go with your gut.** When provoked, don't give in to your first response, which is usually anger or defensiveness. Acting on impulse would give the other person the advantage by causing you to invoke that kind of emotion. Take a deep breath, and consider your next words with care.

- **Slow down.** When we are angry, we tend to speak faster and louder. Make a conscious effort to keep your volume down and your speech steady. If anything, speak just a bit more quietly than normal — doing so forces others to listen more closely and gives you a psychological edge.

- **Call a timeout.** If you are truly angry, put off reacting at all. Say something like, "I am not prepared to deal with that right now, but I'd be happy to speak with you after the meeting." In an article published in HR Communication titled, "Stay in Control When You're Under Attack," this type of response is not avoidance, as long as you set a specific time to revisit the issue. By dictating when and where you will address the issue, you are setting the terms of engagement — which puts you in control.

How else can we have better control over our emotions?

As addressed in many ways in this book, individuals must be more aware of their emotions before they respond. They need to evaluate their feelings and determine the best and most appropriate way of responding. One of the best ways is to consider the things that are within and outside of your control. If there are things outside of your control, it does not make much sense to focus your stress and energy on that as opposed to focusing on things within your control.

Oftentimes, we spend a lot of energy being frustrated and stressed out over things beyond our control. Sometimes we do not realize that we have no control over the situation because our emotions cloud our judgment. Usually the things you are able to control are things that deal with you personally. For example, improving your job performance, increasing your business sales, or improving relationships with your peers, coworkers or family members are all things within your control. Things that you do not have control over are those that affect other people or circumstances. For example, your favorite boss gets replaced by a mean and incompetent boss, or someone else gets selected for a promotion or a job you wanted.

Below is an exercise that will help you identify the types of situations that are within your control. The intent of this exercise is to understand the things you can change and how to deal with the things you cannot change. Once you have this understanding, you can control your emotions more productively.

ACTIVITY 2: IDENTIFYING CIRCUMSTANCES WITHIN AND OUTSIDE YOUR CONTROL

Write circumstances or conflicts you are dealing with within your control in the left column below. Then identify circumstances or conflicts you are dealing with that are outside of your control in the right column. This will help you focus on the things you can control. For example: Personal business success, performance, employee morale, etc. I have provided additional examples below to help you get started.

Circumstances Within and Outside Your Control

Improving your job performance	Someone gets a promotion you thought you deserved
Increased business sales	You just received a new boss you don't like
Improving your relationships with peers and colleagues	Your company is downsizing and you may be laid off

12

DRIVE

> *The beauty of drive is that it is infectious. It can spread to others like osmosis.*

Demonstrating poise is a great tool to use when working with others in today's work environment because it strengthens your relationships with colleagues and leaders by helping you manage your emotions and behaviors to prevent from making poor and impulsive decisions and assuming jerkish qualities. This also helps prevent unnecessary conflict and helps you focus more on getting the work done rather than wasting time engaged in conflict from jerks (and, yes, you could be one of those jerks). As I mentioned in the beginning of this book, we can spend more than two hours per week dealing with conflict from jerks instead of focusing on our work. However, it takes much more than this to succeed in today's work environment.

Throughout life, we will face challenges that may keep us from achieving our goals. In order to succeed, we must continue to move forward despite these challenges. This brings me to the next trait in what I call the "Five Star Traits" — **Drive**. We must have the drive in the face of adversity to overcome the obstacles that come our way. These obstacles include jerks that may keep you from getting your work done or from accomplishing your career goals. As you will discover in this chapter, depending on what drives you, this trait can make you indispensable to your workplace and capable of working with jerks, or it can make you into a jerk yourself.

In this chapter, you will learn how drive:

- Benefits employees by helping them become indispensable in the workplace,

- Helps business leaders cultivate drive in the workplace so they can leverage it to improve the culture, and

- Helps entrepreneurs stay focused to succeed in the face of adversity.

Don't Chase the Money, Chase Your Dreams

Drive is important for all generations in the workplace, especially when we endure obstacles, such as tight deadlines, lack of resources or competing priorities.

> **Depending on what drives you, it can help you either become an indispensable employee, or an unsuccessful jerk.**

Some people are driven by money or status and are more likely to act like a jerk because they are willing to do whatever it takes to be promoted or receive a raise. More than a year ago, I was invited to participate on a leadership panel at my alma mater, Connecticut College, to share some tips about what it takes to succeed in the work environment. A student, who planned to graduate and enter the workforce that year, asked me what advice I would give to her and other future aspiring leaders entering the workforce. My response to her was, "Don't chase the money, chase your dreams." I explained that in my prior leadership experience as an office manager, I came across many people who were driven by money and status. Some acted like jerks and were willing to sabotage others, take credit for others' work, lie, and cut corners to receive promotions. Some people chased down promotions without a full understanding of the responsibilities involved in that promotion or the ramifications of being promoted. They only saw it as an opportunity to make more money and receive an impressive title. It was all smoke and mirrors.

Focusing on the money means you are focused on the wrong thing. Let me be clear — there is nothing wrong with wanting to be promoted or receiving a raise to improve your financial well-being, especially if you believe you can take on that responsibility and such ascension in your career allows you to add more value to the workplace. But when working with others, the drive to make more money at the expense of hurting others puts you on a path that is short lived and often ends in major disappointment — for the employee and the employer. People who chase the money end up being unfulfilled and unsuccessful in their new position for a variety of reasons. Some people eventually end up regretting what they have gotten themselves into. Once they understand what the job truly entails, they realize it is not what they wanted in the first place. They end up regretting that they accepted the new responsibility because it is more demanding, requiring more time in the office, longer hours, and time spent away from home, family, and all other social activities. Chasing the money also puts them at risk of being promoted to a level of incompetence because they lack the skillset needed to excel at their new position. As you recall me sharing in the beginning of this book, I described this very situation as an example of what causes jerks in the workplace. People who scramble up the corporate ladder just to prove they can climb are at major risk of failing in their new position because they lack the necessary experience to do the current job. They were so focused on getting that promotion, they didn't bother to understand or acquire the tools needed to do the job and to do it well.

DRIVE FOR EMPLOYEES

Instead of being driven by the money, promotion or other materialistic, selfish reasons, cultivate your drive to become an indispensable, highly valued employee.

You can do this by having a team first attitude, helping others and having a strong work ethic.

The truly successful people are driven to help others. They do not chase the material things. They are driven to work and succeed for reasons beyond external rewards (like money and status). These people enjoy satisfaction from just purely doing a good job, solving problems or helping others. They are eager to learn, can be counted on in tough situations and remain optimistic when things don't go as planned. This is why these people are highly valued, are easy to work with and are generally not considered jerks.

What makes them indispensable in today's environment is that they are driven to help others succeed, they are driven to add value, and are willing to work well with others toward a common goal. Driven employees believe they can make a difference and help others. They have an undeniable work ethic and can make a great impact on workplace morale through their positivity and productivity. Usually, these types of indispensable employees have leaders who recognize, encourage and cultivate this drive. But what happens when leadership fails to do this? How do these types of indispensable employees remain driven to add value and help others when there is no leadership to help support and foster this good behavior?

Sadly, in the absence of great leadership, driven employees can lose their drive. In one of my employee development workshops, some employees discussed how they may have started out with a go-get-it attitude only to feel defeated when there was a lack of support at the top. As a result, these people became disengaged, saying "why bother?" Instead of helping others, they resorted to doing the bare minimum because they were so frustrated by their toxic environment and the absence of leadership presence to promote good work ethic behavior. When a situation like this occurs, instead of having a "why bother" attitude, employees can take it upon themselves to create a "team first" environment. I recommend the following:

How Employees Can Detox a Toxic Environment

Become a mentor. More experienced employees can take newer, less experienced employees under their wings and show them how to approach the job with a "team first" attitude and strong work ethic. This will help foster the type of drive that helps others in the workplace. This will prevent that newer employee from becoming disengaged in the workplace. It also helps create a work environment where employees are driven to help others. Although some workplaces have formal mentorship programs, employees can take it upon themselves to be informal, career-changing mentors.

Share information. Whether you are a new employee or a more experienced employee, consider how you might share a best practices guide, some lessons learned, stories about your experiences, or other information that can help others in their jobs. This kind of thoughtful and selfless sharing inspires others to return the favor and pay it forward. This creates an environment of teamwork where people will have the drive to voluntarily help others. Employees are more likely to take these steps when the company or organization has a clear mission and a clear purpose despite a leader's lack of support.

DRIVE FOR LEADERS

Leaders who create an environment where employees are driven to help others create a culture of indispensable employees. Employees also enjoy having these types of people in leadership roles because of their people-oriented focus and because they don't have a personal, self-serving agenda. Leaders need to have the right kind of drive because they set the tone for their staff. If a leader has a strong work ethic and has the drive to make everyone around them better, his or her staff will be inspired to have the drive to not only improve but to help others as well.

I delivered a leadership seminar to business leaders in a non-profit organization where I facilitated a session about improving office productivity and morale. Leadership was frustrated and concerned because of the ongoing conflict occurring between the six different departments in the organization; their primary concern stemmed from the conflict's impact on overall productivity. They sought my help to remediate these issues before things got worse. During the session, I recommended that they use the Assess, Analyze, Act method to resolve the conflict.

Assess. Assess the situation and determine the root cause of the conflict. It turns out that there were various reasons for conflict and the reasons were not necessarily related to one another. It was not a specific issue but a much broader issue that had to be addressed across the entire organization. The environment was somewhat toxic and a change of culture was needed.

Analyze. I had the leaders at this non-profit organization analyze the situation and determine how they could improve the culture to where there would be less conflict and better morale. I asked them to identify the traits they valued in their employees so they could recognize the most important characteristics of high-performing employees and how to cultivate that. Without a doubt, most of the leaders at this client organization valued having employees who are team players, who willingly help others, and who have a strong work ethic. This makes them indispensable because not only do these types of employees improve productivity, their positivity improves morale, and alleviates the stress of a leader who may be burdened with addressing employee performance and conduct issues, or may be too focused on other managerial, administrative duties.

Act. How do you leverage these indispensable employees to create a better culture and improve morale? The leaders need to cultivate and reward these indispensable employees who are driven to help others. Remember, these people are not necessarily doing all this good work for a bonus or a promotion, so rewarding them with more money is not necessarily a trend you want to begin. However, recognizing these employees (whether publicly or privately) goes a long way to show how much you value the contribution of individuals while improving the overall culture at the same time. For example, with the non-profit organization, I recommended that they establish "On the Spot" recognition where leaders can recognize employees for outstanding behavior, acknowledging specific incidences in which they went above and beyond the call of duty. I encouraged them to award these employees during all-hands meetings or special office occasions.

Ten months later, the president of the non-profit organization contacted me, raving about how the culture had dramatically improved since our initial workshop. Through their employee award program, they have created a culture of "team first" employees, driven to help others. By publicly recognizing employees, the organization's leaders showed the rest of the staff all the good work being done and inspired others to develop a "team first" approach. Equally important, this inspirational work also weeded out some of the jerks who caused some of the divisiveness. Some of those jerks inherited a "team first" attitude driven to do whatever was necessary to help out. This improved the company's productivity and morale in less than a year. Leaders were less stressed because they did not have to spend the majority of their time having tough conversations to address poor performance, behavior and conduct. Instead, they were recognizing employees' drive to go above and beyond to help others.

One employee at this very same organization took a medical leave of absence. Instead of the supervisor reassigning her workload to the other employees, her teammates took the initiative to support her by dividing up her workload and taking on the additional assignments while she attended to her health. They did not complain, argue or act like jerks. They worked together to get it done, because it's what they would want their colleagues to do for them.

DRIVE FOR ENTREPRENEURS

When asked about the many thousands of failures he had had when trying to create the light bulb, Thomas Edison famously said, *"I have not failed. I've just found 10,000 ways that won't work."* However, there is even more to it than that. As a child, he was thought to be dumb and was told by many of his teachers that he would never be a success because his mind would often wander in class. Many may believe that Edison would not amount to anything because of his failures and how his teachers viewed him. However, what made Edison successful was that he possessed the internal drive to make a difference, despite his failures, perceived inabilities and what critical teachers thought about him.

Entrepreneurs are successful when they have the drive that will help others and make a positive impact in many lives. You will rarely find successful entrepreneurs whose sole focus is to make tons of money. Often times you will discover that money is the result of what happens when you deliver a product that helps others. In fact, as I mentioned earlier, many unsuccessful entrepreneurs fail within the first few years after starting a business because they give up. When they do not make the money they hoped for, or realize it takes more work than originally anticipated to earn the money they hoped for, they decide it's not worth their time. Successful entrepreneurs have the drive to never give up even when they fail because they have a passion to make a difference in people's lives.

So how can entrepreneurs maintain their drive to be successful?

- **Have a clear and specific purpose.** Be clear on what goal you
  want to achieve. (We will discuss this later in this chapter, in
  more depth, when we cover the SMART Goals section.) Create
  a business plan so you can be crystal clear on how you want to
  build your business. Additionally, creating a business plan will
  force you to be honest with yourself about what is truly driving
  you to start a business. Are you driven only to make more money?
  Is it to make a difference in people's lives? Understand why you
  want to build your business before you start it.

- **Read up on other successful entrepreneurs.** Understanding
  what drives other successful entrepreneurs will help you focus
  and will drive you to model the same behavior.

- **Get a mentor.** Having a mentor will help you stay focused and
  help you maintain your drive. Your mentor will serve as your
  accountability partner to ensure you are reaching your mile-
  stones and will help maintain your drive when you are feeling
  overwhelmed, frustrated, or need an assessment.

The beauty of drive is that it is infectious. It can spread to others like
osmosis. You can help others maintain the necessary drive to keep
moving forward when faced with setbacks, adversity, or when things
to do not go as planned. There is perhaps no better way for me to
illustrate the infectious nature of drive than to share a story that is
deeply personal — a story about my own hopes and aspirations, and
about a teenager who changed my view of everything. There was
a time when I was driven by the potential fame and money associated with becoming the Toastmasters World Champion of Public
Speaking. I was virtually obsessed with the idea of making this
happen in my life.

Toastmasters International, as many readers likely know, is
a worldwide organization that helps produce effective leaders
and communicators. At the time of writing this book, I have been
a member of Toastmasters for four years and was the 2015-2016
president of my local chapter. I joined Toastmasters because I was
sick and tired of stuttering and making excuses to not speak each
time my boss asked me to provide an update on my project. Having
the drive to improve my public speaking skills helped me gain the
confidence to speak in public or whenever my boss asked me to. In
fact, this experience inspired me to publish my *Speaking Like a Pro*
eBook, which provides tips and tools to help people communicate
and present information clearly, concisely and confidently, whether
you are speaking in front of a packed audience, briefing your boss, or
presenting information to others.

> For more information on how you can obtain the *Speaking Like a Pro* eBook,
> visit my website at www.TailoredTrainingSolutions.com.

In addition to helping people manage their fear of public speaking,
and improve their speaking skills, communication skills, and leadership skills, Toastmasters allows its members to share stories,
and enriches the competitive spirit through speech competitions.
Toastmasters has an annual international speech competition where
thousands of people worldwide compete to become the world champion of public speaking. I wanted to win badly. I wanted to win to
become the world champion of public speaking.

However, I discovered something more meaningful and more
valuable, and something that was truly life changing through that

competition. I discovered it only when a high school student pointed it out to me.

You see, as it turns out, my speech helped give that student the drive to help others, and *his* success helped me realize that having the drive to help others is worth more than any personal accolade. He changed my view of speaking forever, and he changed how I viewed the results of the Toastmasters International Speech Contest in which I participated ... and lost.

When I entered the contest, my inner voice kept telling me, "You are one step closer to accomplishing your dream of becoming a successful speaker. All you have to do is win this contest and you are one step closer to achieving that dream. You'll change your career, you'll get the speaking engagements, and everyone will recognize you as a successful speaker."

I can think of how past champions of the Toastmaster Speech competition launched successful speaking careers after they won it all, 2012 champ Ryan Avery, 2001 champ Darren Lacroix, and 1999 champ Craig Valentine, just to name a few.

My inner voice kept saying, "I want to get book deals, I want to get paid $10,000 per speech, and I want to become a successful speaker just like them!"

As I ended my speech during that fateful competition, I shook the contest master's hand and proceeded back to my seat. As I walked toward my seat, I quickly assessed my performance: *Did I stutter or stumble over any words?* Nope. *Did I use hand gestures, vocal variety and emphasize important points in the speech?* Yup. *Did I make eye contact and engage the audience?* You betcha! *Did I nail it?* I think so!

In addition, if I needed any more confirmation, I looked no further than the club president at the time. As I performed my speech, I could see him listening and staring at me, smiling from ear to ear. His body language said it all: "You're doing it! Keep going!" Even his eyes lit up while I delivered my speech exactly as I had rehearsed. It reminded me of the movie *Rocky II* when Mickey coached Rocky Balboa to win the boxing title.

I sat back in my seat and my wife whispered in my ear, "Over the last thousand times I heard this speech, you never performed it that way. You nailed it!"

Yup, I nailed it. However, was it good enough? Well, based on my quick assessment, I thought I had a great shot. The contest master stood in front of the audience. My heart raced. My mouth went dry. The room spun a little. As the contest master opened his mouth, I hoped he would not call me first. If called first, that meant I would be runner-up. I took a deep breath in, then out, waiting on his words. As his voice called out over the audience, he bellowed out my name, and disappointment invaded me. I had won the 2nd place trophy. In other words, my deepest fear had come true: My best was not good enough.

My stoic reaction masked the sting of disappointment. I forced a smile. In addition, the competitive spirit within me could not help but wonder how and why my best was not good enough.

The opportunity cost to win that competition meant spending countless hours practicing, rehearsing and dedicating much of my free time to work on that speech. Therefore, to come up short felt devastating and, even more importantly, the inner me felt that I took a step back from accomplishing my goal of becoming a successful speaker. I failed. My best was not good enough. At that moment, I feared

I would not become the successful speaker I had always dreamed and knew I could be.

The sting of losing lasted longer than I expected. However, about a week later, I attended an all-male summit at a local high school, where I had previously conducted a workshop for Junior ROTC students, and I ran into one of the JROTC students who heard my speech when I practiced it during his class prior to the competition.

I barely recognized him in his JROTC uniform because he hadn't been wearing his uniform when I attended his class the first time. But I quickly remembered him because he wore these glasses with thick black frames. He told me how my speech inspired him to enter the school's essay contest. He added that although he hates to write, I inspired him to share his story about constantly being outside of his comfort zone.

He explained that his dad was in the military so he had changed schools at least three times. Because he never settled in anywhere, he found it difficult to find friends. He told me he knew what it was like to feel alone even when surrounded by classmates and he does not want others to feel that way. He felt that by sharing his story, he would help others who feel alone or are bullied by other students.

Wow. Talk about a stunning moment!

I felt embarrassed, a little ashamed, and kind of like a jerk. I'd been moping around for a week, thinking that my second-place finish meant that my speech didn't matter. I thought that my "miss" at fame and fortune meant that my words hadn't made a difference to anyone. But I was wrong; I've never been so happy to be wrong. That young man made me realize that my speech did, in fact, make a meaningful impact. It actually drove *him* to help others. I was humbled.

Although I did not win the speech competition, I won something more far-reaching and valuable. I won insight about what I really care about — helping others be their very best. That is what really drives me, and now I finally understood that.

* * *

What drives *you?* Is it to be a great coworker? Is it to be a dynamic leader? To be a team player? I realize that we may all be driven by different things.

The reality is that your drive seldom goes unnoticed and your actions may inspire someone to make a positive change in their life. And to me, that's worth more than any personal accolade. Will I enter another speech competition? Certainly. However, winning or losing will have no impact on my success as a speaker.

> **The ability to inspire others is what validates my speeches.**
> **I know what drives me.**

The next time you take action on something, especially in the work environment, keep in mind your actions may influence others to have the drive to perform better, become a better teammate, better leader or entrepreneur.

MAINTAIN YOUR DRIVE WHEN FACED WITH FAILURE

People who lack drive will most likely give up on themselves, their jobs, teammates, and anyone else who supported them. Some people lose their drive when they get frustrated when they don't meet their own expectations. When they face this type of failure, they give up and stop trying. To overcome this adversity, like many successful people do, use failure to drive you to succeed.

Like some of you, failure helped me find the drive to succeed. Like most people, when I was a kid, I had dreams and aspirations. Like others, I wanted to be someone and do something special. Back in the day, you could ask my mom who I'd be and she would say, "My baby's gonna be a lawyer. He's always giving people advice at such a young age, especially when no one asks for it."

I made the local paper one time for winning a chess tournament. When the reporter asked who I wanted to be, I responded, "A lawyer." When asked why I said, "So I can get good people out of trouble, help people in need, and say things like, "Objection, Your Honor! He's guilty!"" I was in awe, watching lawyers on TV with their flashy suits and dramatic speeches. In addition, nobody did it better than Perry Mason. Thanks to him, I won the biggest argument out of my childhood years. (I convinced my friends that He-Man could beat the Incredible Hulk in a fight.)

Growing up in New Haven, Connecticut, there were three options when finishing college: A.) Get a job, B.) Go back to school, or C.) To the chagrin of some Millennials, move back in with your folks.

My folks made that decision very easy on me. They said, "If you think you're going to live back home with us – you better pay rent!"

Option B, it was! I was going to law school. But there was only one thing standing in my way. One annoying, little obstruction. And I couldn't get past it.

Me!

That's right, I didn't need anyone to get in my way ... I could do that on my own. Studying? Please!

Others relied on good test scores to get into school. But I had a secret weapon. Something that not many people possess. Something that set me apart from everyone else — a killer smile! That's right, I just needed to flash these dimples and I was a shoo-in.

It was a warm autumn afternoon when I received my first letter from a potential law school. I couldn't wait to open it.

> *Dear Mr. Williamson:*
>
> *Thank you for your interest in our school. After completing a careful review of your application and supporting credentials, our Admissions Committee has concluded that we are unable to offer you acceptance to the program ...*

**Not one, not two, but 19 rejection letters? Really?!
Clearly, they didn't see my killer smile.**

What's worse than letting myself down? Letting my mom down. I could've done better; I should've done better.

I'll never forget the day I broke the news to her — I felt so guilty telling her. She greeted me at the bottom of her old wooden steps.

"Mom, I want you to be the first to know — I didn't get in." I could barely look at her. "I just wanted you to be proud."

What was I going to do now? I needed a pick-me-up. And I did what anyone in my situation would do. The only thing that made sense. I watched the movie *Rocky* — the perfect feel-good movie for inspiration.

As I surfed the net, I came across a story about the actor who played Rocky — Sylvester Stallone. You won't believe what I read. It changed me forever. According to the story, Stallone tried to sell his screenplay, *Rocky*, to producers. He was rejected more than 50 times. He was so poor he had to sell his best friend, his dog, for $50.

Finally, months later, someone loved the screenplay and offered him $100,000 for the movie. Stallone said, "I'll accept under one condition: I have to play Rocky."

The producer declined. He said, "Stallone, you're not an actor."

You won't believe what happened next, Stallone declined their offer! Can you imagine what the producer did? He raised the offer to $400,000! That was good money back then — even today! Would you believe that Stallone still declined? The producers finally gave in and said, "Stallone, you can play the lead role, but we're only giving you $25,000." What Stallone did was unprecedented — he accepted!

We all know this movie was a huge success, winning three Academy Awards. Stallone was persistent, determined and resilient, but that's not what I admired the most. I admired his passion. He found something worth pursuing and did not let anyone or anything get in his way. I wished I had that drive. Stallone inspired me to find my own drive. Being a lawyer was not it. I wanted it for the wrong reasons. I didn't put in the effort. If I did, I would not need this killer smile. I would have taken the test seriously and tried again.

Those 19 rejection letters remind me of a time when I was mentally lost. I was angry at those law schools and jealous of the people who went there. I was angry with myself because I didn't know who I wanted to be. That's something I couldn't live with. I had to make some changes.

WRITE DOWN YOUR GOALS

It started with taking responsibility for my actions. I was living based on other's expectations. I had to take control of my life. I remembered what my mom told me as a kid. She said, a dream is just a dream. But when you write it down, it becomes a goal. So I wrote down these words: "Pursue my passion." I had to do more than just say it, I had to write it — I had to own up to those words. And it paid off. By writing it down, my dream became a goal — a goal to help others who were lost like me. Similar to the failure I felt when I lost the Toastmaster's competition, I realized I could use this experience for a greater purpose to help others. To that end, I am giving people a chance at a better life. I'm providing leadership tools to keep employees poised for success. Through mentoring, coaching and training, I've helped a public sector administration become one of the top 10 places to work for six straight years, creating stronger teams, better working relationships, and improving morale. I've helped people achieve their goals and pursue their passion, helping people advance and flourish in their professional careers.

I've started a successful company and my mom and dad have never been more proud!

Your story can be anything, but will you be your own author? Is there something in your life that you want to change? Be the author of your own destiny. Find what drives you, then pursue your passion!

To find what drives you in order to pursue your passion, you need to be specific and crystal clear with what you want. I recommend using the SMART Goals frame to achieve that kind of clarity. Below is high-level overview of how to make your goals "SMART;" for a deep-dive and a thoughtful discussion about how to craft SMART goals and why they matter, I strongly suggest Rajib Lochan Dhar's book *Strategic Human Resource Management.*

SMART GOALS: SPECIFIC, MEASURABLE, ATTAINABLE, REALISTIC, TIMELY/TANGIBLE

Specific

Ask yourself these simple questions:

- **Who:** Who is involved?
- **What:** What do I want to accomplish?
- **Where:** Factor in logistics.
- **When:** Establish a time frame.
- **Which:** Identify requirements and constraints.
- **Why:** Specific reasons, purpose or benefits of accomplishing the goal.

Measurable

| *"Goals are dreams with deadlines." — Diana Scharf*

After you have narrowed your goal into something more specific, then ask yourself these questions to measure your progress, ensure your success, and make sure your goals are still on track.

- How do you know that you are achieving your goals?
- What does success look like to you?
- Establish criteria for success: Use concrete numbers in your goals so you know if you are staying on track or need to make changes.

For example, if your goal is to lose weight, how much weight do you want to lose? 10? 20? 30 pounds? Or you may want to be more descriptive. Your goal may be to fit into the jeans you wore when you were 18 years old.

Track your progress. If your goal is to lose 15 pounds in six weeks, but you've only lost two, you may need to rethink your strategy. Keep a journal to track your progress, efforts, results, and feelings about the process.

Attainable

Make your goals tangible and attainable. Consider the obstacles you have identified and the challenges you have encountered. Is it reasonable to attain your goals based on these obstacles? Is it reasonable to assume you can overcome your challenges?

Consider the length of time it will take to achieve your goals. What circumstances will delay or challenge your goals? For example, if your goal is to start your own business, it will be a lot more attainable if you break it down into smaller steps. You may not be able to build your business in a day, but completing your business plan within a few days is much more attainable and specific. This method makes the process much less overwhelming and daunting.

When you identify these obstacles, you can then use the points you have read in this book to help you find solutions to overcome them — whether the problem is lack of money, skills or abilities. An ideal goal is one that is within reach, if only you can stretch and grow and challenge yourself to get there.

Realistic

A realistic goal must be something you are both *willing* and *able* to work toward. This does not mean that setting low goals are the only way for it to be realistic.

For example, for the majority of my adolescent years, my goal was to become a lawyer. Once I did some self-reflection and asked the question, "Why do I want to be a lawyer?," I realized that it would not make me happy. And I didn't ask myself that question until after I'd applied to law schools and failed to get in. Of important note: Make sure you consider how your goal fits with other plans in your life to make sure you have no conflicts. Does it fit into the rest of your life's plans? Being realistic means being honest with yourself about what you can accomplish and whether now is the right time.

Timely

Speaking of time, what is one of our most valuable commodities? Time! A goal with no timeframe is not a goal worth pursuing. If your goal doesn't have a timeline for completion, you may be wasting your precious resources. You should have a sense of urgency. For example, if you want to write a book, when do you want it published? Set clear timelines for your goals (e.g., "I'd like to have the book in bookstores in March of 2018"). Setting a timeline for your goal keeps you accountable for taking the specific actions necessary to accomplish your goal. If you have no timeline, you have nothing to strive toward, and nothing compelling you to continue pursuing it.

Break your long-term goals into smaller goals (What's the best way to eat an elephant? One bite at a time.) This will help you manage your progress much better. For example, if your goal is to write a book in five months, you can set a goal to write at least a few pages each week. This makes the process more manageable and less overwhelming. It also gives you confidence to move forward with something to strive for. Ask yourself the following questions below:

- What can I do today to reach my goal?
- What can I do during the next three weeks to reach my goal?
- What can I do across a longer period of time to reach my goal?

Focus more on consistency and stability. Adopt habits that will keep you focused on your goal.

SMART GOALS ACTIVITY

Here is your chance to construct a roadmap to pursue your passion and fulfill your dreams! Complete your action plan by establishing SMART Goals.

Think about your passion, something you want in life, whether in your professional or personal career and write it down. Consider any workplace or professional challenges you are having that you want to resolve.

_____

_____

_____

_____

_____

Now, complete the SMART Goal activity to outline how you will pursue your goal.

Specific:

_____

_____

_____

Measurable:

_____

_____

_____

Achievable:

_____

_____

_____

Realistic:

_____

_____

_____

Timely/Tangible:

_____

_____

_____

13

PERSPECTIVE

If you can't change circumstances, change your perspective.

Although having drive can make you indispensable in the workplace and is necessary to overcome obstacles and setbacks, one of the most important traits needed to overcome obstacles and resolve conflict with others is perspective. Perspective is the ability to acknowledge the emotional diversity in others and respect their feelings even if we have not experienced what they are experiencing. This fourth trait among the "5 Star Traits" involves a true understanding of someone else's point of view.

In this chapter, you will learn how perspective:

- Empowers employees' ability to understand someone else's point of view and lead without having the title

- Helps leaders retain talent, improve workplace morale, and connect with others and

- Assists entrepreneurs in being able to effectively serve their clients and customers.

Having perspective is a trait that is deeply lacking not only in the workplace, but in our personal lives. Sometimes we take it for granted. It is one of the foundation blocks of learning that allows us to understand and respect one another. It is pure and authentic, and its value cannot be overstated in the workplace. Similar to empathizing with someone, with perspective, you don't have to go through the same experience as another person, but you *do* have to seek to understand how they feel and how you would feel if you were in their situation. You may not know what it is like to speak English as your second language, for example, but imagine how lost you would feel if you couldn't communicate with anyone in your native tongue. That ability to imagine is perspective.

GAINING PERSPECTIVE WHEN YOU STEP OUTSIDE OF YOUR COMFORT ZONE

I used to have a comfort zone where I knew I couldn't fail.
The same four walls of busy work were really more like jail.
I longed so much to do the things I'd never done before.
But I stayed inside my comfort zone and paced the same old floor.

I said it didn't matter that I wasn't doing much.
I said I didn't care for things like diamonds, furs and such.
I claimed to be so busy with the things inside my zone,
But deep inside I longed for something special of my own.

I couldn't let my life go by just watching others win.
I held my breath and stepped outside to let the change begin.
I took a step and with new strength I'd never felt before

I kissed my comfort zone good-bye and closed and locked the door.
If you are in a comfort zone afraid to venture out,
Remember that all winners were at one time filled with doubt.

A step or two and words of praise can make your dreams come true.
Greet your future with a smile ... success is up to you!

– Author Unknown

STEP OUTSIDE YOUR COMFORT ZONE!

Having perspective compels us to step outside of our comfort zone
and do something we are not used to doing. In order to step outside
of our comfort zone, we have to be willing to be in uncomfortable
situations. Author and speaker T. Harv Eker said it best when he said,
"Nobody ever died of comfort, but living in the name of comfort has
killed more actions, more ideas, more opportunity, and more growth
than everything combined. Comfort kills!"

One of my most memorable experiences with gaining perspective
forced me to step outside of my comfort zone. It helped shape my life
to what it is today. In 2001, I travelled to Costa Rica during a study
abroad program. This was a significant moment in my life because it
allowed me to appreciate a perspective I would have never achieved
staying home. By living in another country, I learned what it was like
to feel completely vulnerable, surrounded by others who represented
a different culture, who lived a different way of life, and who spoke
a different language than I do.

I can remember when I was on the plane to Costa Rica, and when
reality set in. I thought to myself, "What did I get myself into?"
I remember I had this small Spanish dictionary with me on the
plane. I figured all I had to do was translate a word I did not know
in order to get by. I was sitting next to a Costa Rican man who was
speaking Spanish to me. I could not understand what he was saying
and I could not sift through the words in the dictionary fast enough

to understand. I was getting scared. Fear and doubts crept all throughout my body. I kept thinking to myself that I was in way over my head. My parents were thousands of miles away. I was alone.

I can recall the first morning when I went to my first Spanish class. This was an intermediate Spanish class for non-Spanish-speaking students to learn the basics. The inner me looked forward to attending this class because I saw it as an opportunity to learn Spanish so I would no longer feel uncomfortable with my host family or meeting new people. My host mother handed me the school address. She tried her best to explain that it was a straight walk for a few blocks. I thought I understood what she was saying and, for some reason, I felt confident about finding my destination.

Before l left the house, my Costa Rican mother said with the warmest smile, "Adios, que le vaya bien, y dios la acompañya!" I looked at her with confusion on my face. I did not know what she meant. I did not realize that she was wishing me well on my journey to school and for God to be with me. I just replied, "Adios," and began walking to school. As I walked, the inevitable happened: I got lost on my way to school in a foreign country! I panicked! I walked frantically up and down the streets. Everything looked the same! I couldn't read any of the names of the streets or other signs, nor the business names. The more I walked, the worse it got!

I eventually stopped walking and turned to my right to see a guard who was standing outside a bank holding a shotgun. I was scared! Not just because I couldn't speak Spanish, but because he was holding a big shotgun in his hand. But I had no choice ... I had to reach out for help and find directions to my destination. I was trembling and sweating profusely as I approached him and uttered, "Yo no soy...donde esta?" Although that little bit was the most Spanish I had ever spoken, I felt proud that I could utter those words.

However, I did not make any sense. The guard looked at me as if I was crazy. Then he clutched his weapon even tighter! I walked slowly backwards. I realized that I had to ease a situation that started to escalate rather quickly. Thankfully, I remembered one word that the person on the plane ride to Costa Rica told me that could get me out of this situation. "Ayudame!" I regrouped, and approached him again, and shouted, "Ayudame! Ayudame!" and pointed to the address of the school hoping that he would draw the connection that I was lost. He looked down at me, looked back at the address written down on my piece of paper, opened up his mouth and said in English, "Gringo — the school is two blocks up to your left."

Although this seems pretty funny looking back on this experience, it was not so funny at the time. I was lost in a foreign country and the guard was intimidating. But as I look back at this experience, it has made me less fearful of the unknown and more confident in my abilities. Living in Costa Rica was beyond my comfort level at first. I was afraid, I was nervous, and I felt incompetent. Because I could not speak the language, I felt inadequate and inferior to others.

I gained perspective on how difficult and challenging it can be for some people who speak English as their second language, or others who feel like an outsider or like they don't belong. This experience helped me when I took on future leadership positions. As a business leader, this experience helped me become more compassionate and embrace diversity in the workforce. It also helped build my perspective when helping new employees who have ever felt vulnerable getting acclimated to a new environment — whether it's a new employee reporting to work for the first time, a recently promoted employee or supervisor acclimating to a new role, or someone who is taking on a new work assignment for the first time.

The Costa Rican perspective helped me communicate more effectively with Spanish-speaking customers while gaining a better understanding of some of the vulnerabilities they experienced and the communication challenges they endured when visiting my office to seek assistance. Some Spanish-speaking customers who came into the office had difficulty communicating with the employees because most could not speak Spanish. I knew how vulnerable they felt. I could relate to them through my Costa Rican experience.

Looking back, I was glad that I had the opportunity to learn from an uncomfortable situation. That Costa Rican experience helped me grow as a person and achieve the perspective needed to deal with conflict and build better relationships with coworkers, staff and clients.

PERSPECTIVE FOR EMPLOYEES

For employees, your ability to have perspective with others and comprehend what others have experienced can and will generate success in the workplace. Without perspective, you will alienate people and never know why. It is difficult to succeed without having perspective. This is true for entrepreneurs or employees working for a company. Without perspective, you will be unable to produce a desired result or draw a connection with others. Part of the reason is because relationships will suffer, which makes it harder to get work done. No matter how skilled we are, we rely on others (including jerks) to get our work done, whether it's to make photocopies or to get buy-in on a particular course of action on an assignment. When we lack perspective, employees may not feel understood or respected in that environment. They may have resentment and are not likely to want to work with you.

HOW EMPLOYEES CAN USE PERSPECTIVE TO LEAD WITHOUT THE TITLE

Employees can apply perspective in a variety of ways in the workplace. Most notably, employees can apply perspective when it comes to working with newer, less experienced employees. In one of my "How to Work with Jerks" workshops, I led a session with employees to show them how having perspective gives them the power to improve employee morale and office productivity without having to leave it in the hands of their management. During the workshop, some employees expressed frustration about how their management lacks the ability to address performance issues for some of the newer staff. This has forced the more experienced staff to take on additional workload because the newer employees are unable to handle their full workload. The management seemingly turns a blind eye because the work is getting done; they're not concerned about *how* it gets done.

Although it is true that, ultimately, the buck stops with the office manager to resolve office problems, I explained to the employees in my workshop that just by having a perspective on the situation, that they hold significant power to make a difference, and shouldn't always have to rely on the office manager to resolve their issues. The employees were frustrated not only in the manager failing to address the performance issues with the newer employees; they were also frustrated that the newer employees were not producing their fair share of work. Employees can resolve this type of issue by showing perspective in the following ways:

- **Pause**. Take a step back and think about what it was like to be a new employee. What were some of your challenges? Did you have support from other coworkers? Did you have resources available to help you get acclimated to the job? What helped you improve? Once they thought about how it felt to be a new employee, they not only thought about some of the useful ways that helped them get acclimated, but they also came up with other ideas to help the newer employees do their jobs better.

- **Support.** Meet regularly with team members *without* management. This allows the employees to have a discussion about courses of action for projects and assignments, and to prepare for upcoming meetings. This encourages a safe environment for employees to get on the same page with a particular course of action, discuss challenges with particular work assignments and possible solutions to those challenges. It also helps the newer employees better understand their roles and responsibilities. Provide resource guides and material to help them not only get acclimated, but to be self-sufficient.

- **Connect.** *What if you cannot relate to their situation?* Some students have asked me how they can gain perspective with others in the workforce when they have not experienced that specific situation. One of my recommendations is to think back on prior experiences you have had either personally or professionally that can be used to connect to other people's experience. For example, I used my Costa Rican experience to help me gain perspective with employees who have felt vulnerable being in a new environment or people who had difficulty communicating in a different language.

These measures help the employees bond together and address work issues as a team. It also shows that employees don't have to have a leadership title to lead change. They have the power to lead change by using perspective to connect with their colleagues, helping improve productivity and relationships within the office.

I revisited this same company to conduct a follow-up workshop a couple months later to assess the situation, and I was happy to learn that they followed my advice. I found out that the employees created a "best practices guide" for new employees to help them get better acclimated to their jobs. The guide includes resources for processing certain workloads, points of contacts, and writing guides. They also established a mentorship club through which more experienced employees mentored the newer employees. The office morale had improved, the productivity had improved and the newer employees were taking on more share of work.

By having perspective, the employees were motivated to help their fellow co-workers adjust to the office. They felt a sense of empowerment to address these issues head on without relying on their boss's help. Not only did the experienced employees feel motivated to help the less experienced staff, but the inexperienced staff felt encouraged and supported.

HOW PERSPECTIVE CAN PREVENT LEADERS FROM BECOMING JERKS

Employees may consider leaders who lack perspective to be, simply, *jerks*. And as you all know by now, I can relate all too well to what it's like to be a jerk. According to many people I have met along my professional career, pretty much everyone can relate to the experience of having a jerk in their midst. They universally agree that it's a problem in the workplace that has been plaguing us for a long time. Just about everyone who has ever worked knows what it's like to work with a jerk, and it seems to be getting worse, affecting countless people each day.

What makes someone a jerk? Is it because they are control freaks, are they too bossy, do they blame others when things don't go as planned, or take all the credit when things go well?

All of these things may be true, but it really boils down to perspective. A jerk is someone who lacks perspective toward their employees; he or she is someone who fails to see the workplace through their employees' eyes, fails to understand the challenges of others, and refuses to make changes when necessary to accommodate others.

When I was an employee, I told myself that if I ever was promoted, I wouldn't be a jerk, and that I would appreciate the people who worked for me — until I became ... a jerk. It is not like I woke up one day and aspired to be a bad boss! It just happened!

The weird thing about it was that I didn't even know what I was doing wrong. I was clueless. I realized that all the good work I did as an employee had nothing to do with being a boss. It did not matter if I was once the best worker bee in the office because, as a boss, I was responsible for making sure everyone else did the work.

The further I was removed from that work, the more I lost sight of what it was like to be one of them. We looked at work through different lenses. We talked past each other. Even worse, I forgot what it was like to be in their shoes and understand the stress and challenges that they dealt with each day while still getting the job done.

The only thing that mattered to me was meeting our company goals — and pleasing *my* boss.

Because of this disconnect, our relationships on the team suffered and within six months, so did our performance. My lack of perspective killed their morale and made it a bad place to work.

To make matters worse, my boss paid me an unexpected visit to assess the mess I had made! Even though she was barely five feet tall, she was very intimidating — she never smiled. She stared at me with this stern look and pointed her finger as she spoke. "I travelled over 100 miles to see this mess for myself. I am beginning to doubt you have what it takes to run an office. Either show some improvements, or I will find someone else who will!"

I felt demoralized and defeated. Didn't my boss *understand* what I was going through as a new manager? Wasn't she aware of all the challenges I had to overcome?

As I left work that day, I ran into the security guard. He was a retired city cop who loved to tell stories about his days patrolling the streets. His stories usually began with the words, "Back when I was about your age ..." He must've seen the pain and frustration on my face — it was impossible to hide. "Bad day?"

At first, I didn't feel like talking but, deep down, I needed to get my feelings out. The words began to flow. "My employees don't like or respect me, and my boss is going to fire me if I don't improve. I don't know where I went wrong. I didn't have these problems before I got promoted — when I was one of them. They now look at me like I don't get it, like I don't understand them."

He paused and stared at me with his hands on his hips before replying, "Back when I was about your age, when I first started out as a cop, people in the neighborhood felt the same way about me. But one day, I sent a little boy home who was caught stealing food, rather than send him to jail. It showed them I had perspective about the hardships of an ailing single mother, whose only son tried to keep them from starving. I guess what I am trying to say is, 'people don't care how much you know, until they know how much you care.'"

Those words changed my whole outlook. I spent the weekend thinking about my situation at work and how I could turn things around. I spoke with my mentor, who gave me some advice. My mentor helped me realize that I needed to establish a relationship with each of my employees. I needed to get to know them personally. I decided to hold one-on-one meetings with each of them. That would give me the opportunity to learn and gain perspective about what they are working on, determine their challenges and offer support. These meetings would also allow the employees to see I am approachable. They could ask questions, present concerns, etc. In addition to the one-on-one meetings, I wanted to build trust as a unit. I organized some team-building exercises to build trust and strengthen our relationships. Some of the team-building exercises involved sharing one or two unique and interesting things about each other. I figured that knowing more about each other at a personal level would help us all understand how to work better and more cohesively.

I returned to work with a renewed passion and a different focus. Instead of worrying about making the company goals, I gained perspective about the *people* doing the work.

Not only did our relationships drastically improve, but so did their morale and our performance dramatically improved in the end too.

This was life changing. Perspective goes beyond the workplace. When we take the time to listen and acknowledge what people are truly going through, it makes our lives much easier and it builds relationships.

Nelson Mandela said it best when he said, "What counts in life is not the mere fact we have lived. It is what difference we have made in the lives of others that will determine the significance of the life we lead."

I challenge you to make a difference by gaining perspective of others because, in the words of Theodore Roosevelt (and our wise security officer),"Nobody cares how much you know, until they know how much you care."

PERSPECTIVE FOR WORKPLACE LEADERS AND ENTREPRENEURS

In the workplace, perspective is important to practice because it helps you develop a better understanding and appreciation of someone else's experience, allowing you to form meaningful relationships with coworkers and leaders. Whether you are a manager, leader or executive, relationships are particularly important because you are evaluated based on getting work done through other people. Your success and effectiveness is directly related to your ability to motivate others to get the work done. As a leader in the workplace or an entrepreneur who has employees working for them, it is important to inspire and motivate others, especially when there is low employee morale. Perspective can boost morale. When employees know that their leaders value them and understand what they do is important, and when they feel recognized for their efforts, employees will have more respect and trust in their leadership. They are more inclined to work harder for their leader.

What happens when you deal with someone who lacks perspective? As I explained in the personal story about what happened when I lacked perspective toward the people I managed, it creates a toxic working environment and can demoralize a team. For example, during one of my workshops a client was seeking advice about how to create a more productive work environment. She was a director and she described her work environment as a place where there was more work than people to do the work — which was stressful enough. Her staff consisted of new employees mixed with some veterans who were nearing retirement. As a result, production suffered and she was challenged with doing more with less. She was frustrated because she felt her staff was not stepping up to meet her expectations. She told me that she thought she was doing the right things by giving them feedback, stating what they needed to do to improve on or what they needed to do more of in order to meet her expectations. However, that didn't improve their production. In fact, it got worse. She decided to carefully review their work to make sure they were not only doing it right, but exactly how she used to do it when she was an employee. That still didn't work and she noticed her staff's attitude began to change. She noticed the low morale. She wanted my advice on how to turn things around.

Based on my prior experience as a bad boss, I could relate to her situation all too well. I started talking to her about the importance of perspective. Her environment is already stressful enough with the amount of work her staff has to complete. But what she failed to realize was that half her staff members were new and inexperienced and needed additional support and time to get acclimated. I worked with her on some techniques to build perspective through the AAA (Assess, Analyze, Act) technique:

1. **Assess.** Assess the situation and check the temperature of the staff. If morale is low and you are not getting through to them, identify the triggers that cause this to occur. What challenges are you dealing with?

2. **Analyze**. Seek to understand and reflect on the situation. How are the employees responding to those challenges? In this situation, the director is challenged with doing more with less in a workplace with low morale. The director must not only meet the daily tasks but also motivate and equip the staff to get the work done. In this situation, the challenge was not only doing more with less, but working with inexperienced staff and others ready to retire with one foot out the door already. She could analyze this situation by gaining perspective and looking **through their lens**. I told her to imagine when she was a new employee and how she struggled. I asked her to recall the times she needed help from others. I told her to think about how her new employees feel being new to the job. They need similar guidance, training and support as she needed when she was in their shoes.

3. **Act.** After analyzing the situation by showing perspective, the director was more positioned to address the issue. By thinking back to her time as a new employee, she recognized how

vulnerable her current new employees may be feeling and, thus, acknowledged that they may need support and a boost of confidence. I recommended that she practice doing the following:

- **Give small wins**. This means giving balanced feedback and not always focusing on the negative. By giving recognition and acknowledging her staff's efforts, it will motivate them to work harder and do a better job. I asked her how she would feel if she constantly received feedback on what she was doing wrong and what she needed to do better.

- **Empower, rather than micromanage**. When she micromanages, she acts like a jerk because it shows her staff she doesn't trust them and they may feel hesitant or afraid to do their work without her correcting them. Staff may feel inadequate, unappreciated and incapable of meeting their boss's expectations. Instead, empower them to get the work done. Empower the experienced staff to mentor and help the newer members get the work done. How would she feel if she had every aspect of her work carefully examined without the latitude to take care of the most routine tasks? Empowering others shows a level of trust and responsibility that takes time and experience. Empowering others to do certain things or make decisions is something that should not be taken lightly nor should you expect it to happen immediately. It takes time to trust someone enough to empower them. A good leader develops trust. A leader must know that you are capable of handling particular assignments or making certain decisions. That person must be competent and capable, and this trust occurs over time and with experience working together.

I explained to this client that bosses who fail to change their behavior and show perspective will lead a toxic and unproductive work environment causing resentment and hostility. The new staff may leave for another job and the more veteran staff may retire earlier than expected.

Change may be difficult for both employees and leaders. But it is incumbent upon the leader to have the perspective to make necessary changes in leadership style to lead a productive and stress-free work environment.

In the article titled, "What Leaders Really Do," John P. Kotter, a retired professor of organizational behavior at Harvard Business School says, "What leaders really do is prepare organizations for change and help them cope as they struggle through it." He continues by describing the challenges leaders face when trying to produce change. "Leaders almost always have had opportunities during their 20s and 30s to actually try to lead, to take risks, and to learn from both triumphs and failures. Such learning seems essential in developing a wide range of leadership skills and perspectives. These opportunities also teach people something about both the difficulty of leadership and its potential for producing change."

Leaders must be effective in leading change in their organizations. In order to effectively lead change, leaders cannot expect a change in an employees' behavior or a change in results if leaders *themselves* are not willing to change. Many people are unwilling to change out of fear of doing something outside of their comfort zone. It takes courage to change, and courage can be hard to muster. It also takes deep reflection and having a perspective to understand and accept that change has to begin *within* before you can change others. For example, if you are trying to help your employees become more productive by achieving certain workload goals, you cannot expect this change to happen overnight or occur unless you are willing to make some changes in your leadership style by motivating your staff, reallocating resources, or taking a hard look at whether your productivity expectations are realistic.

Business leaders, employees, and generations of all types must have perspective. It is one of the best tools you can use to resolve conflict. Make every effort to understand what someone is going through in order to build communication and draw a connection. In today's fast-paced world with emerging technology, one thing that cannot and must not be replaced is the human element of understanding and gaining perspective of others.

Perspective in the workplace is extremely important because it:

- Improves employee morale
- Shows you care
- Improves business productivity
- Improves work relationships
- Improves employee retention
- Reduces unnecessary conflict
- Empowers staff.

PERSPECTIVE TIPS: A SUMMARY

To practice perspective with others in the workplace, I recommend the following tips:

1. **Seek to understand and reflect on the thoughts and points of view of others.** Once you are able to understand another point of view, you will have a better perspective of the entire situation, which will help you resolve the conflict effectively. Try putting

yourself in someone else's shoes. How would you react if you were in that person's situation?

2. **Active Listening**. A key component of perspective is listening. Really listen to the other person's perspective and hear the entire message. Actively listen by asking questions, confirming your understanding and clarifying anything that does not make sense. Give that person your full attention so they can open up and be completely honest with you. Give them the reassurance that what they have to say is important.

3. **Empower, don't micromanage**. Giving people latitude is gratitude. Empowering them to get the work done instead of leading every detail of the assignment will go a long way. It builds trust, respect and accountability. People will be more engaged and are more willing to participate in work activities.

4. **Provide small wins**. This boosts the confidence of others. Don't always focus on the negative. While it is good to communicate expectations and ways to improve, also provide balanced feedback and words of encouragement. This will motivate others to get the job done right and work more effectively to meet expectations. Newer staff need to have confidence that they can and will eventually get the job done right. Acknowledging the good things they do will help cultivate their ability to learn and improve.

PERSPECTIVE ACTIVITY

Consider the traits that make someone a good boss or a bad boss. What about them did you like or dislike? We recently surveyed employees and had them identify what makes someone a good boss or a bad boss. Most said that a bad boss is a micromanager, but a good boss empowers. Do you feel the same way? Answer the questions below to provide your input.

Identify at least one person in your life who has micromanaged you.

_____

_____

_____

What qualities made him or her a micromanager?

_____

_____

_____

_____

_____

_____

Identify at least one person in your life who has empowered you.

_____

_____

_____

How did they empower you?

_____

_____

_____

_____

_____

How did it make you feel to be empowered?

_____

_____

_____

_____

What was the result of your empowered actions?

_____

_____

_____

_____

What makes someone a good boss?

_____

_____

_____

_____

_____

What makes someone a bad boss?

_____

_____

_____

_____

_____

Applying Perspective to Deliver a Better Message

Sometimes messages can get lost in translation based on how they are delivered. The intent of the message can be interpreted the wrong way when we lack perspective. Think back to a time where you received or delivered an email or had a discussion that may have been misinterpreted. By applying perspective, determine how that message should have been received.

Example: When submitting a work assignment for a presentation, Jim received the following email from his boss:

"The work you submitted for this presentation did not hit the mark. Fix it and submit it again."

If you were Jim, how would you feel about receiving this email? How would you apply perspective to understand or justify the supervisor's reasoning for sending this message? If you were his supervisor, how would you apply perspective to convey more constructive feedback?

Now, it's your turn!

Identify a situation where you received or delivered a message that did not come across as intended. What was the result of the situation? How could you have applied perspective to deliver (or receive) a better message?

_____

_____

_____

_____

_____

_____

_____

_____

_____

_____

_____

_____

_____

_____

_____

_____

_____

_____

_____

_____

_____

_____

_____

_____

_____

RAPPORT

> *"Rapport is Power"* – *Tony Robbins*

Perspective is one example of how leaders and employers can improve overall workplace morale and professional relationships. Rapport is equally important and a powerful tool to build networks with colleagues and influence others to get things done in the workplace. The average person spends 8 or 9 hours at work each day (and some of us spend even more); as such, it's imperative that we build meaningful connections with the people at work. Building rapport helps you make friends, build allies and navigate through politics in the work place, but it is more than that. Rapport is about finding common ground and working toward an end goal. For someone to succeed in today's work environment, you must establish rapport with all types of colleagues, especially jerks. Whether you are an employee, entrepreneur or a leader within your company, you must be able to manage relationships, build networks and establish rapport, as these are the keys to long-term success.

In this chapter, you will learn how rapport:

- Empowers employees to have a say in the workplace and help implement change,

- Helps leaders use rapport to create an environment of trust and better manage employee performance, and

- Helps entrepreneurs use rapport to create an environment of trust

According to Tony Robbins, rapport is created by a feeling of commonality. People like people who are like themselves (or who have something in common with who they would *like* to be). To that end, you can establish rapport by mirroring others in the following ways:

- Using the same tone of voice
- Using similar vocabulary or jargon
- Matching the same gestures
- Making sure your breathing is in sync

People who build rapport with others are able to collaborate with others, influence decisions and, most importantly, lead change.

HOW LEADERS BUILD RAPPORT

In addition to the above examples, I recommend leaders build rapport in the following ways.

Three Up, Three Down

Leaders can build rapport with their employees when it comes to managing performance and building trust through providing fair and honest feedback. But not just any type of feedback will do. It must be specific feedback that's also balanced and constructive. Some leaders believe that only pointing out the areas where an employee needs to improve upon will lead directly to improved performance. The Baby Boomer generation may relate more to this type of feedback because, to them, this sort of "tough love" is part of a hard day's work.

Unfortunately, Baby Boomers have become accustomed to seldom receiving pats on the back. But in today's multi-generational environment where relationships matter more than ever, and where employees are increasingly empowered to have a say in their career development, focusing only on what an employee can improve upon (or what some call "focusing on the negative") can ruin rapport between a leader and his or her staff.

When leaders focus exclusively on the negative, they come off as jerks, and employees can end up feeling defeated — as if they are not capable of doing their job effectively because they're constantly being told what areas they need to fix. An employee is also more likely to tune out their boss and be disengaged in the discussion if they feel like their boss is being too negative. If a leader continues to focus on the negative performance issues, an employee may get fed up to the point where they refuse to cooperate with their boss's guidance for improving, feeling there is no hope to meet their boss's expectations, so why even try?

Instead of emphasizing the negative to the exclusion of the positive, leaders should take a more balanced approach. I conducted a leadership seminar with a group of managers and I shared with them a technique that will help them build rapport with their staff and ensure performance discussions go much more smoothly. This technique, called the "Three Up, Three Down" approach, was first introduced to me by Laura Liswood in her book titled, *The Loudest Duck.*

The "Three Up, Three Down" approach is a method for balancing both positive and negative feedback when leaders hold performance discussions with their employees. Leaders are encouraged and sometimes challenged to identify three pieces of positive feedback if/when there are three pieces of negative feedback. This balanced approach is effective because it allows for a productive two-way conversation. Months after the workshop, some of the leaders contacted me to report that practicing this approach has created stronger relationships with their staff. The leaders reported that employees were more engaged in their performance discussions and understood what they were doing well and things they needed to improve upon. Some of the leaders from the Baby Boomer generation realized that their employees were more likely to feel encouraged and motivated to improve when they acknowledged some of the good things their staff have done. These leaders also reported that their staff members have since been more likely to improve their performance because they feel that they are being supported — that their boss genuinely wants them to succeed.

This approach to balanced feedback also alleviates some of the stress when a boss has a difficult performance discussion with an employee, because when a boss acknowledges some of the good things an employee has done, they are able to build a stronger relationship and establish common ground. The employee is less likely to take the negative feedback personally and will be less defensive because the employee is more apt to accept the feedback as honest and fair.

How Leaders and Entrepreneurs Build Rapport with New Employees and Colleagues

When there are new employees in the office, leaders and entrepreneurs can and should establish immediate rapport with them. There are, however, some people in leadership positions who fail to build rapport with others in the workplace. Some leaders don't always take the time to know the people who are working with them — especially if they are new to the organization. In the flurry of a busy office setting, some leaders simply don't prioritize taking the time to meet with the new person on the team to establish rapport and set clear expectations.

Whenever a leader receives a new employee, it is absolutely necessary to do the following to build rapport and get off on the right foot. I recommend doing the following:

Meet with the person and set clear expectations. What do you expect from the employee? Advise him or her of any cultural protocols or company etiquette around how they are expected to work with you and with others.

Provide training. Identify available resources to help with learning gaps.

Communicate more in person vs. email to prevent things getting lost in translation.

Some leaders, sadly, continue to act like jerks — choosing to lead through fear rather building rapport with their staff. Even the smartest and most talented leaders can fail to build rapport and take advantage of opportunities to build relationships with their staff. As a result, they are unable to find out what motivates their staff and they miss a wonderful opportunity to not only learn about the people they lead, but to learn vital lessons about themselves. If leaders don't take the time to learn about their employees, they will have a hard time getting their staff to embrace change, step outside of their comfort zone or feel motivated enough to perform at their very highest levels. To that end, things will not change; there will be no room for creativity or growth. People will be uninspired. People will leave your organization.

HOW EMPLOYEES BUILD RAPPORT WITH OTHERS

In one of my teambuilding workshops, I helped employees build better rapport not only with their coworkers, but with their management staff — something not many of them thought was possible. One employee who recently got hired at a new job was frustrated that her boss didn't offer an opportunity to telework. She worked for a supervisor who valued the traditional working environment, where you show up to a physical, shared workspace five days a week. She expected her staff to report into the office each day and she was not a proponent of flexible working options — also known as teleworking or telecommuting. For her, she needed her employees to physically show up to work because that was the only way she would know for sure that they were doing their jobs. She was driven by a need to control and by a lack of trust in the people who reported to her.

Although the company had a policy that permitted teleworking, that policy could be applied at the discretion of the supervisor. Most, if not all, of the supervisors in the company, except for the one particular woman's supervisor, allowed their employees to telework weekly.

Here are the top three reasons why this group of leaders supported telework:

1. It fosters work/life balance,
2. It saves time spent on the road, in traffic, and saves money spent on gas,
3. It eliminates distractions in the workplace that we take for granted.

The employee's previous assignment allowed her to telework every day, and she loved it. Therefore, when she transitioned to this current job, she was disappointed that her team did not telework. She asked her teammates why they had never been allowed to telework and they responded that nobody asked the supervisor and the supervisor never offered them that option, although they were interested in the possibility. She was in a dilemma: She was new to the job, so was it really her place to confront her supervisor and request to telework? She didn't want to step out of line or get off on the wrong foot with her supervisor. She was new to the job, after all, and she didn't have any established rapport with her boss. She was hesitant to even bring up the topic for fear of what her supervisor would think: "How dare she challenge my authority like that?!"

During our discussion, I could tell that she was aggravated because she wanted to telework, but didn't want to jeopardize her standing in the office. But by using the AAA Method, she was able to use the power of rapport to address the situation and get her desired result that ended up being a win-win for everyone.

1. **Assess**. She assessed the situation. Although she was grateful for her new job, she was frustrated that her team wasn't afforded an option to telework. She missed that perk from her previous job. She was aware that she was the new person on the team and didn't have an immediate rapport with her teammates or her supervisor. She was also aware that teleworking was permitted in

the office because other teams in the organization were allowed to telework.

2. **Analyze**. She considered waiting for her six-month review before she requested teleworking because, by that time, she would have earned her stripes, established better rapport with her supervisor and colleagues, demonstrated her work ethic, and would be better positioned to make the request. I asked her, "What if you waited six months only to find out that she fully supports teleworking and probably would have supported it if you asked her earlier? Wouldn't you feel upset that you let all that time go by because you were waiting for the right time to ask, when you could have been teleworking had you asked her earlier?" And conversely, I also asked her, "What if you waited the six months only to find out that she would not allow teleworking?" She agreed she would be upset given either scenario, and realized that there was no benefit in waiting. She realized she would be better off speaking about it sooner rather than later.

3. **Act**. In order to have that conversation with her supervisor took careful planning. It was important that she didn't come off abrasive or entitled (i.e., she didn't want to be perceived as a jerk). We talked about the power of rapport and how getting buy-in from her team can help influence the outcome of the situation. She established rapport with her teammates by meeting with them and learning that they all had something in common — they all supported teleworking as an option, for themselves and for their peers.

Next, she established rapport with her supervisor. Once she got her teammate's support, she took it a step further and anticipated what her supervisor would need before she decided to talk to her. She anticipated that her supervisor would want to see a teleworking schedule before agreeing to anything. She developed a teleworking schedule based on feedback from her teammates. She met with her supervisor to discuss the feasibility of teleworking. Her supervisor's response was that she was unaware that people wanted that as an option and that when she was with her former employer, there were strict rules for teleworking. Even though she was in a new company that fully supported it, and had a liberal teleworking policy, she was hesitant to try employing the policy at work. She was afraid to break from the norm. All her life she was used to commuting and showing up at work, and she expected her staff to do the same. Once she realized that her staff wanted to telework and had a schedule for teleworking to alleviate any concerns about lack of office coverage, she agreed to allow it. Once the team began teleworking, the employee morale improved and they completed their work more efficiently.

LESSONS LEARNED FROM BUILDING RAPPORT

Both the supervisor and the employee learned some valuable lessons from this experience. The rapport they built from that meeting created a stronger relationship (as well as trust) between the supervisor and her employees. Instead of responding like a jerk, the supervisor embraced the power of rapport, which helped her feel more comfortable adjusting her management style to allow teleworking. In the beginning, she expected her employees to commute to work just as she had. However, she learned that she could be a more effective leader (and less of a jerk) by listening to the needs of her employees and being open to change.

As for the employee, she learned to build a stronger relationship not only with her coworkers, but also with her boss. She garnered trust with all of them and was the catalyst in influencing a decision that would allow them to telework. By building rapport through listening and communicating with her boss and colleagues, she helped lead change that benefited everyone.

Whether you are an employee or a leader, taking the time to build rapport with the people you work with will help you draw a deeper connection with others, which will improve morale and productivity in the office. Your coworkers will appreciate and respect you for taking the time to get to know them and build true relationships instead of doing the opposite and acting like an everyday work jerk.

Rapport Tips

Below are some tips for building rapport with colleagues:

- **One-on-Ones.** These meetings usually occur with a supervisor and employee or just with team members. One-on-one meetings between a supervisor and employees allow both parties to discuss expectations, concerns, issues or status on projects. One-on-one meetings with fellow coworkers allow both parties to get on the same page with projects and also create a good environment to mentor, if needed. These meetings also allow for a comfortable environment where people can feel safe to discuss work-related or personal issues that affect their work. It's not unusual for employees to broach important topics in one-on-ones that they would not discuss in any other environment.

- **Be Emotionally Curious.** Effective managers should connect with their staff on an emotional level and show interest. Ask them open-ended questions, such as, "What was the best part of your day and what was the worst part of your day?" or "What personal passion project are you currently working on right now?" Managers should be *emotionally curious* and demonstrate that by being interested and by asking questions. Dale Carnegie once said, "To be interesting, you have to be interested." A great way to be more interested in people is to ask them open-ended questions. Get them talking about themselves to build rapport.

RAPPORT ACTIVITY

Follow the steps below to build rapport the next time you are in the workplace:

1. **Mirror the other person.** Observe their body language and try to mirror it. For example, if they fold their arms or cross their legs, you do the same (though don't be obvious or creepy about it!). Use similar body language. If they appear engaged, comport your body so it matches the same level of engagement. You can also mirror how someone sounds or how they dress.

2. **Use good communication.** Communicate politely and show respect. Be sure to practice active listening so it shows you are engaged.

3. **Find common ground.** Think back to the story of the new employee building rapport with colleagues by coming to an understanding that they all wanted to telework.

Common ground is a great place for relationships to grow.

---

4. **Practice perspective** (refer to the Perspective section for details). See things through the other person's point of view so you can try to relate to the other person and understand them better. Try on their shoes, see through their eyes, challenge yourself to step out of you own unique position and into theirs.

15

CONCLUSION

As my mentor once told me, it's not about the work, it's about the people.

> At the core of our profession, no matter how talented, gifted or experienced, and no matter what role we serve or title we carry, our level of success is not measured based on the work we produce; it is measured based on the relationships we build.

Whether we realize it or not, we rely on others to succeed. What makes it difficult to achieve that success is when we have to work with jerks. As mentioned in the beginning of this book, work jerks are people who fail to use social skills and the ability to connect with others as a necessary job skill. Whether people refuse to leverage social skills or are unaware of their value in the workplace, lacking these skills makes it extremely difficult to be your very best at what you do.

You may recognize some characteristics of jerks as being rude, bossy, sarcastic, narcissistic and prone to micromanaging. A jerk may also be someone who steals credit, is a poor listener, poor communicator, inflexible and/or creates a toxic environment based on fear and distrust, and much more. Some of us may think that only other people are jerks, but I encourage you to be introspective and consider for a moment whether you have acted like a jerk in the workplace or are acting like one now. Most of us have no intention of acting like a work jerk, but may find ourselves doing so when we lose sight of our purpose, get stressed over workload demands and are faced with tight deadlines, or are completely outside of our comfort zone and have no experience in a particular situation.

Before leaving you to tame the jerks in your life, let me review with you on last time the four primary factors that can cause otherwise well-meaning individuals to become jerks at work:

1. **Ongoing frustration caused by social media and technology.**
    Although meant to make our lives easier and more efficient, these tools and the habits they create can work against us and cause jerkish behavior when interacting with others. It's important to not lose sight of the human element in the workplace. So put down the phone, stop reviewing email and give your coworker their full attention!

2. **Ongoing anxiety caused by lack of training and preparation.**
    When we are hired into the workforce or receive promotions or reassignments, we are outside of our comfort zone and may be unprepared for what awaits us. Whether you're a student who just graduates from college and is entering the workplace for the first time, or are a seasoned professional recently hired into a leadership position, you may have no idea how to adopt the necessary socials skills needed to manage workplace relationships or how to navigate through the political atmosphere embedded in the work environment. As a result, you (or people in similar situations) can come off as rough around the edges and unable to connect with others.

3. **Insecurity caused by financial uncertainty.** Volatile economic times create a level of stress, anxiety and desperation for individuals — the uncertainty includes everything from fear about losing their job due to layoffs, to anxiety about slashed budgets, fewer staff to help carry the load, or the possibility of wage freezes and evaporating bonuses. People can lash out over frustration dealing with the thought of facing setbacks and having to start over again. Conversely, economic insecurity can cause people who are poised to retire to remain employed to make a living for their family. (This too can cause people to lash out and act like a jerk because they are unable to retire. Imagine feeling ready to move on, but unable.)

4. **Continuous stress due to a lack of generational awareness.** Today's diverse, multi-generational work environment can create toxicity and misunderstandings when we fail to acknowledge or adjust our working style to effectively communicate with fellow coworkers. The greatest opportunities exist in our differences, if only we can understand, respect and flex to make those differences work in our favor — individually, as teams and as organizations.

In the end, work jerks are problematic because they can affect your company's bottom line as well as your health and wellbeing. Dealing with jerks can be stressful because we can spend so much time dealing with conflict from jerks instead of getting our own work done. Dealing with this conflict can cause us to not show up to work. In fact, 25% of employees who don't show up to work do so to avoid working with jerks. And when we eventually show up to work, we have to confront these jerks, which can lead to workplace conflict or even violence. When people who get fed up and leave the company due to working with jerks, it costs employers nearly double that employee's salary just to find a replacement.

The way we disrupt the process of becoming work jerks is by implementing both **the AAA Method: Assess, Analyze, Act** and the 5 Star Traits.

The AAA Method is a three-step process to help you strategically deal with conflict and address tough situations in the workplace. Avoiding jerks, telling them off, or committing violent acts are not good solutions; negative responses to jerks make you become a jerk yourself and ultimately make the situation worse.

The next solution is the 5 Star Traits. It's no secret that we will need to interact and communicate effectively with all types of people to get things done. To do this, we will need a flexible set of skills to diffuse tense situations, manage conflict and alleviate stress when dealing with others, especially jerks.

The Five Star traits — Recognition, Poise, Perspective, Drive, and Rapport — should be used when dealing with people in the workplace, regardless of their title or profession. These traits reflect what we need in today's multi-generational work environment, where people feel over managed and under led, to improve production and work better with our colleagues, especially jerks. I encourage you to leverage these traits in all aspects of your work when dealing with others. These traits will benefit everyone around you as well. You can use the basics of this model anywhere you go in your career. These traits should not be recognized as something nice to have — they are essential. We are evaluated based on how well we are able to interact with others, especially in management, where technical skills are less necessary, and leadership and people skills are required.

These traits are in all of us and we have the potential to use them and develop them at any time. This is the case because it's in our nature to see the good in people and to treat them with compassion, respect and dignity.

We don't always get to choose the people we work with. We do, however, get to choose how we handle the relationships with the people we work with — especially the people who we can't stand (or who can't stand us). Recognition, poise, perspective, drive, and rapport are traits that we have thoroughly examined in this book and are tools that will arm you to get work done when dealing with jerks at work or people who may possess jerkish qualities anywhere in your life.

No matter your role or title in the work environment, I urge you to practice humility and don't ever allow your ego to become your amigo. Be thankful for the tremendous opportunity and responsibility that comes along with working with others. Appreciate the people you work with because you will need their help at some point. Without them, you cannot have success in the workplace.

SOME FINAL LESSONS, AND FAREWELL

For leaders, remember that your title alone will not make employees respect you or follow your lead. But if you have the drive to help others, and create a positive, healthy work environment, your team will be driven to succeed. Detox your office space by earning and keeping their respect by employing the 5 Star Traits. This will help create a stronger relationship with your staff, and will promote a healthy work environment, boost morale and build leaders you can be proud of.

Employees, you don't have to have a leadership title or a corner office to make an impact in the work environment. Success today is not just about how smart you are, but how well you can work with others and control your emotions. Building allies across the organization helps you accomplish your work goals, and nurturing these relationships will make the workplace and tasks more enjoyable, increasing your overall job satisfaction and the opportunities that will be afforded to you.

Your emotions and the emotions of others can affect nearly everything you say and do each day. How you deal with these situations can predict your performance and determine your success. These tools are the strongest drivers of leadership and personal excellence.

I hope this book has encouraged you to leverage these tools personally and professionally. As you can see, the benefits are overwhelming, from receiving promotions, raises and financial freedom, to strengthening our relationships with others, helping us work better together and gain a better understanding of each other. And these days, we can all benefit from that. There is no such thing as a perfect leader or employee. We must all learn from our experiences, mistakes, failures and successes. Learning is an iterative process and I encourage you to continue learning and becoming a better person so that you can work well with everyone and help promote a jerk-free environment.

Thanks for reading.

ABOUT THE AUTHOR

Eric L. Williamson is the president and
CEO of Tailored Training Solutions,
a small business that works with
organizations that want to create an
environment where employees are
engaged, appreciated, and developed into leaders. Eric is a keynote
speaker who is often referred to as the
"Connector" for his ability to make
his message resonate with groups, or

as the "Change maker" for his ability to inspire change and improve
morale by coaching people to bring out their very best. He is known
for his empathic, engaging, down-to-earth style. Eric's fusion of
real-life stories and his conversational techniques connect with his
audience at an intimate, intense and individual level.

Eric's desire to see others improve, survive and thrive in the workplace is what drives him to help others succeed. He has delivered
motivational speeches and programs to businesses and organizations throughout the country. He helps professionals at all levels to
take steps to improve their workplace relationships with all types
of people in the work environment ... especially the ones who are,
let's face it, jerks.

Eric earned his bachelor's degree from Connecticut College in 2002, and his MBA at the University of New Haven in 2008. He lives in Maryland with his wife and daughter, and is eagerly awaiting the arrival of a second child at the time of publishing this book. Eric loves to grill food outdoors no matter the weather. He enjoys salsa music and loves to go salsa dancing. When he's not working, he's often vacationing at the beach with his family. This is his first book.

REFERENCES

Brack, Jessica. n.d. Kenan-Flagler. https://www.kenan-flagler.unc.edu/executive-development/custom-programs/.

Bradberry, Travis. n.d. *Success.com*. www.success.com/article/why-you-need-emotional-intelligence-to-succeed.

Castro, Amy. 2016. *Gov Exec*. February 2. www.govexec.com.

Dunkel, Tom. 2014. *AARP*. April. http://www.aarp.org/politics-society/advocacy/info-2014/the-generation-war.html.

Gilles, Gary. n.d. http://study.com/academy/lesson/what-are-baby-boomers-definition-age-characteristics.html.

Goldman, David. 2009. *CNN Money*. January 9. Accessed January 9, 2009. http://money.cnn.com.

Goleman, D. 1998. *Working with Emotional Intelligence*. New York: Bantam Books.

Haiken, Melanie. 2014. *Forbes*. January 12. Accessed January 12, 2014. www.forbes.com/sites/melaniehaiken/2014/06/12/more-than-100000-suicides-tied-to-economic-crisis-study-says/#14039d781cbb.

Hyder, Shama. 2013. *Forbes.* December 6. www.
forbes.com/sites/shamahyder/2013/12/05/
study-reveals-surprising-facts-about-Millennial
s-in-the-workplace/#55f2c0da12be.

Kotter, John P. 2001. *Harvard Business Review.* December.
www.hbr.org.

Patton, Meiko. 2016. *Careers in Government.* July 9. www.careersing-
overnment.com.

Schawbel, Dan. n.d. Payscale. www.payscale.com/data-packages/
generations-at-work.

Singular, Stephen, and Joyce Singular. 2015. *In the Spiral Notebook:
The Aurora Theater Shooter and the Epidemic of Mass Violence
Committed by American Youth.*

Smith, Jacquelyn. 2014. "8 Things You Need to Know About
Millennials at Work." *Business Insider.* November 18. http://www.
businessinsider.com/what-you-should-know-about-Millennial
s-at-work-2014-11.

2016. "Stay in Control When You're Under Attack." *HR
Communication.*

n.d. Talentsmart. http://www.talentsmart.com.

White, Doug, and White Polly. 2015. *Entrepreneur.* July 28. https://
www.entrepreneur.com.

ACKNOWLEDGMENTS

Aside from raising a family, this book has been the most challenging thing I have ever felt so passionate about doing. For the past two years, I have put my heart and soul into this book. Doing so would have been impossible without the people who supported and encouraged me along the way. These people were vital to my success, personally and professionally. They believed in me and I will never forget that. A few of these amazing people are listed below.

Thanks to my Mom, Dad and sister. You always knew I had it in me to do something special that would benefit people in need. Your love, guidance and support inspired me to be who I am. Because of you, I was able to write this book. You instilled in me hard work and perseverance, and helped me turn failure into triumph. I know I will never be able to repay you for everything you have done for me in my life, but just know I am forever grateful and will always love you.

My thanks to Michael Davis, the Storyteller MD, for your mentorship and guidance for several years during my professional speaking career. Because of you, you have helped me deliver stronger speeches. Most notably, you referred me to my author coach Cathy Fyock when I needed help with my book — the best decision I ever made. Michael, you provided me guidance and insight when you didn't have to. And that is saying a lot ... it's hard to find people so genuinely helpful.

A sincere thanks to my author coach Cathy Fyock. Reaching out to you was the best decision I ever made. Not only did you guide me in the right direction for writing, publishing and marketing my book, you introduced me to a whole new world of awesome authors and professional speakers who have shared their knowledge and wisdom throughout this journey. Without your support, I would have rushed to publish a book that simply wasn't ready. Your skills and expertise are beyond reproach and I strongly recommend that any author, new or experienced, seek you out as their author coach.

A heartfelt thanks to Kate Colbert and the team at Silver Tree Publishing. Your knowledge and expertise go far beyond the publishing realm, and your thoroughness and attention to detail helped me produce a professional high-quality product. Your unwavering support and guidance provided a sense of calm during a very hectic time. I had a terrific experience with you all, and if asked to describe Silver Tree Publishing in a word, it would be CLASS! Your publishing company is second to none and made me feel part of the family as you attended to my every need as an excited new author. I appreciate how timely you were in all you did and that, above all, you and your team CARE!

Many thanks to my clients. I will always be grateful for your insight and support, and for the opportunity that you afforded me to make an impact and provide tools people need to improve professionally and personally. I have learned so much from you and I continue to do so. I will forever be grateful to you for trusting me with your business.

A special thanks to my editorial board, Michael, Daniel, Bianca, and John. Your insight and feedback helped me produce an important book that everyone will benefit from. You helped me deliver a far greater product than I ever could have imagined.

Thanks to Toastmasters International. I originally joined this organization to speak more confidently and concisely when delivering presentations for work. Who knew this organization would inspire me so much to begin my speaking career. I will always be indebted to this organization for its ongoing support and I will continue to be a member and help others along the way.

A special thank you to everyone I have worked with along the way, jerks and all. My experience working with you helped me learn what to do and what NOT to do in the professional work environment. Every experience is a learning experience. I have learned so much from great mentors along the way, including those whose leadership styles I did not always agree with. For better and for worse, I learned greatly from each experience, and that learning has helped me become a better leader, entrepreneur and person.

A loving thanks to my daughter, Sophia. I thought writing a book would be hard, but it doesn't compare to being a father. Although you may not fully realize it, you have challenged me to dig deep, prioritize and complete this book with an added degree of difficulty to make sure my princess is happy and taken care of.

To my unborn son, Jaxon. By the time you are born, I will have officially become an author. Something I didn't think possible. Let this be an example that you can do anything if you are determined and focused.

And lastly most significantly, thanks to my wife, Aleah. I couldn't have written this book without your guidance and inspiration. I've asked so much of you and I am forever indebted to you for everything you have done. Because of you, I am a successful author, entrepreneur, husband and father. I love you.

74936184R00108

Made in the USA
Middletown, DE
01 June 2018